REGIONAL DIVERSITY

A Joint Center Outlook Report

REGIONAL DIVERSITY

Growth in the United States, 1960–1990

GREGORY JACKSON
GEORGE MASNICK
ROGER BOLTON
SUSAN BARTLETT
JOHN PITKIN

with a foreword by
DAVID T. KRESGE

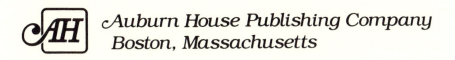
Auburn House Publishing Company
Boston, Massachusetts

Library of Congress Cataloging in Publication Data
Main entry under title:
Regional diversity.

Includes index.
1. Economic forecasting—United States. 2. Population
forecasting—United States. 3. United States—Economic
conditions—1971–   . I. Jackson, Gregory, 1948–
HC106.7.R346   338.5′443′0973   81-12768
ISBN 0-86569-107-X   AACR2

Printed in the United States of America.

FOREWORD

Growth in the United States has always been dispersed unevenly
among the different regions of the country. But as the national
growth rate has slowed in recent years, the contrasts among regions have been sharpened. Older manufacturing areas have
slowed their growth, or in some instances even declined, as industry and households have continued to move toward the southern and western states. That trend is likely to persist through at
least the next decade according to the analysis presented in this
volume, the Regional Outlook Report of the Joint Center for Urban
Studies.

The projections in this Outlook Report indicate that the dispersion in regional growth rates observed during the 1970s will,
if anything, widen during the 1980s. The fast growing South Central and Mountain regions held less than one-fourth of the nation's
population in 1980, yet are projected to account for more than
60 percent of U.S. population growth to 1990. The Mountain
region alone, the smallest of the nine Census regions with just
5 percent of U.S. population, is expected to account for 17 percent
of the national growth.

In sharp contrst, the urban industrial states in the Mid-Atlantic
and East North Central regions are expected to suffer population
losses as young persons move to the "Sunbelt" seeking jobs, older
persons move there to retire, and low fertility and immigration
fail to offset these losses. Industrial decentralization, rising energy
costs, and changing family structures and lifestyles are some of
the factors contributing to this movement out of the older manufacturing centers. These forces are likely to persist for some time
yet, causing these regions to continue showing little growth in
economic activity and population through the 1980s.

Other regions will show similarly diverse, though less extreme,
growth patterns in the coming decade. The authors see New

England, for example, as a resurgent mature economy that is now building on its new areas of strength (electronics, medical care, and so on) after having gone through a difficult period as its older industries (shoes and textiles, for example) moved to the South or to foreign countries. The South Atlantic region, having grown rapidly during the 1970s, is expected to decelerate sharply. There is evidence that the recent strong growth in the South Atlantic region has begun to push up labor costs in these states, thus limiting the region's ability to attract new industry at the same rate as in the past. Perhaps more important, the retirees moving toward congenial climates, who previously had converged on Florida, are now spreading out among a number of other areas such as Arizona and Southern California.

The overall picture emerging from this Regional Outlook Report is thus one of considerable diversity, both in the rate of regional development and in its composition. The demographic analysis in this report draws heavily on and is an extension of the national materials in the Joint Center's 1980 Outlook Report, *The Nation's Families: 1960–1990*. The Outlook Report series encompasses all three of the Joint Center's major research areas: housing and construction; regional and urban development; and family and population studies. Each year an Outlook Report is published in one of these areas to bring together the findings of recent Joint Center research and to discuss their implications. A Housing Outlook Report will be produced in 1982 to examine the prospects and problems for regional housing markets in the coming years.

The Joint Center for Urban Studies, established by MIT and Harvard in 1959, addresses the research and policy needs of an increasingly complex urban society. The Center's mandate is to conduct research in urban and regional affairs, to build a bridge between fundamental research and policy applications, and to strengthen the educational program at the two universities. The Outlook Report series makes an important contribution to the Joint Center's program by making the results of its research more readily available to a wider audience.

Many individuals assisted the authors with the research underlying *Regional Diversity* or with the final production of the volume. Scott McDonald, Randy Crane, Betsy Churchill, William Trigg, John Pflieger, Jr., and Sara Nesson served as research assistants for different parts of the analysis. Cheri Minton translated a variety of regional comparisons into computer-generated maps using programs made available by Harvard's Laboratory for Computer Graphics. These maps helped the authors grasp differences more easily; two appear in Chapter 3. Glenna Lang prepared the figures and graphs which appear in Chapters 2, 3, and 4. Carol Scanlon nurtured the final manuscript as it evolved from rough scribblings, with the assistance of Jan Lent, Irene Goodsell, Angie Ferreira, and Chris Gunlogson. Finally, Charlotte Moore supervised most of the publication process.

DAVID T. KRESGE
DIRECTOR

CONTENTS

LIST OF FIGURES

LIST OF MAPS

LIST OF TABLES

REGIONAL DIVERSITY

Chapter 1

THE NATION'S REGIONS

Two kinds of articles about regional differences appear regularly in *The New Yorker,* both written by Calvin Trillin. The first kind is about an occurrence in a smallish town, often a crime or an urban-development proposal. The second kind is about food. Much is written about the cultural homogeneity and political heterogeneity of the United States, and thus one might expect the former kind of article to emphasize differences among regions and the latter to emphasize similarities. In fact, the reverse is true. Trillin's accounts of eating across the United States suggest that regional differences are intricate, widespread, heartfelt, and enduring; his accounts of small political occurrences suggest precisely the opposite. To oversimplify, Trillin describes a nation in which tastes vary from region to region, but social processes do not. We do not allude specifically to this distinction in what follows, but it underlies much of the regional diversity we describe and project.

Differences among regions have had profound effects on the history of the United States. The northern colonies, which were heavily commercial and headed toward industrialization, and the southern ones, which were heavily agricultural, did not agree on the virtues of independence. The former wanted independence in order to be free of trade restrictions; the latter did not, since England was an important market for cotton and tobacco. Thus the political ramifications of regional differences were strong. Following independence these differences continued, and the steady economic bickering among the newly confederated states led the framers of the Constitution to prohibit, in Article I, the levying of duties or tariffs by states or groups of states. They reserved for the federal government the right to regulate commerce among the states.

1

As the United States has grown and prospered, regional differences such as these have continued to influence the nation.
Historically, for example, the regions of the South supported the
War of 1812 and the Mexican-American War; similar differences
were reflected much more starkly in the War between the States.

Until the mid-nineteenth century there was little actual migration among regions, and thus traditional loyalties to homeland
reinforced regional identities. As new territories opened and improved transportation (railroads and steamships) made migration
easier, regional differences began to reflect individual economic
choices rather than political traditions. The major symbol of regional differences since the late nineteenth century has been
migration, both to newly opened territories and to the economically attractive industrial parts of the country. The gradual change
in these migration patterns, which we describe later in Chapters
2 and 3, has been accompanied by power shifts. North, South,
and West are still struggling over regional differences, which continue to have ramifications for the development of the nation.

Political differences are not the focus of this report, important
as they are. We focus on the economic and demographic attributes
of regions, tracing changes in relation to those in other regions.
We have entered a historical period in which growth in one region
is often at the expense of decline in another. This contrasts with
earlier periods when immigrants to the United States accounted
for much growth, or when older regions invested and therefore
shared in the growth of new regions. (This investment bought
older regions power over the new regions, of course, power which
was bound to end when the latter gained political strength.) It
is thus not possible, given this interdependence, to consider each
region as a separate entity, cataloguing strengths and weaknesses
and projecting change. Instead we must consider the important
elements of national growth and change that are parceled among
regions and assess the forces that cause them to distribute one
way rather than another. The three elements we discuss most—
population, employment, and income—have flowed disproportionately among regions, and these flows are the basis for our
analysis of regional outlook in the 1980s.

Regions are of course in different places, and this fact has profound effects. Historically, four regional features have been most
important: terrain, which influences land use and determines the
availability of inexpensive water power; geology, which through

topsoil affects a region's ability to feed itself and through underground structures determines its underground water supplies and nonrenewable fuel reserves; access to navigable waterways, which until quite recently determined a region's commercial viability; and climate, which influences the costs of agriculture, urban maintenance, and living and constrains lifestyles. Over time the relative importance of these features has changed. Access to waterways, for example, became less important as railroad and later highway transportation became available and economical. Terrain and climate will become more important in some regions as population and economic growth outstrip natural, cheap, or convenient supplies of necessities, such as water or energy.

It is thus no historical accident that the nation's steel and auto industries are concentrated in the East North Central region; its grain farming in the West North Central region; its produce farming in California and the South Atlantic; its financial and insurance institutions in the Northeast; and its energy producers in the West South Central, Mountain, and Pacific regions. In each case the requirements of the business in question—materials in the case of steel and auto; climate and terrain in the case of agriculture; communications in the case of finances; and resources in the case of energy—lead to regional differences. Other industries, which do not have strong regional ties, are more widely dispersed. Regions prosper when local industries or businesses do well or when prosperous national industries or businesses increase their local activity. They suffer when the opposite trends occur. Local businesses that depend on local prosperity, such as retailing and many services, suffer accordingly. This suggests that regional differences must be analyzed in economic terms—that is, industrial mix, "business climate," resource availability, market accessibility, labor supply, and other such indicators.

Some of these factors are exogenous: They are determined outside and independent of the economic system. Raw-material supply (but *not* cost) is perhaps the best example. Others, such as energy supplies and transportation, are partly exogenous and partly endogenous: The factors themselves respond to economic forces. Thus ports, railroads, pipelines, and highways are developed partially because of business or industrial requirements in a particular area. Such interactions work both ways, however. Building highways, for example, changes the costs and benefits of doing business in a particular place and therefore influences economic activity. Social factors, such as business climate, labor supply, and certain market attributes, also interact strongly with economic activity. The major influences here are the numbers, attitudes, and behaviors of individual people. These, in turn, are heavily influenced by individual economic circumstances, which are in turn influenced by regional economic activity, and so on.

If all regions were equally prosperous, or if some regions could prosper without cost to others, regional differences would be of only academic interest (here costs include not only actual losses, but growth substantially slower than national growth). For much of the nation's history the latter statement was roughly accurate. The early settlement and development of the West benefited that region without serious adverse impact on the older regions; in fact, New England invested heavily in the development of the West and profited accordingly. In recent decades this has not been true. As economic growth has slowed nationally, economic expansion in one region has frequently been linked to economic decline in another. The most striking (if not entirely generalizable) example was the development of textile industries in the South at the expense of New England. Moreover, national economic trends and international affairs have disproportionate effects on different regions. For example, a reduction in real income (the result of prices that increase faster than incomes) leads consumers to purchase fewer durable goods, which in turn hurts regions where in consumer-durable industries are major employers. Similarly, as individuals monitor their expenditures more closely, they are increasingly likely to consider regional attributes such as energy costs and to migrate away from regions with high costs of living to less expensive regions—or at least to regions that promise higher incomes to match higher costs.

In this volume we analyze two important aspects of regional difference in some detail. We structure our analysis around population, since demographic shifts are a significant cause and striking consequence of economic differences. We augment the demographic analysis with an examination of related economic trends, particularly regional differences in employment, labor-market participation, industrial mix, income, and wages.

Sharp differences in regional growth rates have been the rule throughout the last two decades, and there has been considerable debate about the near-term future. Standard projections of regional attributes have assumed, for the most part, that growth-rate differences will diminish. However, since they posit different timetables for this, the specific projections vary considerably. Chapter 2 presents our somewhat divergent view of the future. We believe that many of the forces causing regions to grow differently now are likely to persist, at least through the next decade. Our analysis involves both the detailed structure of demographic change and the economic forces that influence it. Chapter 3 delves somewhat more deeply into regional demographics, concentrating particularly on flows and growth rates over the last two decades and attending to the early indications from the 1980 Census. Chapter 4 deals primarily with economic trends, examining historical shifts in regional industry mix and the convergence of regional per-capita income (which is total income, including wage and non-wage components, divided by total population). Chapter 5 takes up the analysis presented in Chapter 2 but concentrates more on the implications of these regional differences.

"Region" is an ambiguous term, both in theory and in practice. There are, roughly speaking, four levels of regional aggregation we might consider for the United States. The first and smallest is the immediate metropolitan or rural area; the Census Bureau calls these "places," and they are typically reflected in postal ZIP codes, telephone area codes and prefixes, and similar regional identification schemes. (Cambridge, Newton, Chelsea, and Watertown are "places" around the Joint Center; Daly City, San Francisco, and Redwood City are places in northern California.) A second, slightly larger aggregation is the economic area, such as the unit defined by the Bureau of Economic Analysis in the Department of Labor. (The Boston and San Francisco areas are examples of such units.) A similarly sized but differently defined unit is the agricultural area, the criterion for which is not economic dependency but climate, terrain, and irrigation similar enough for meaningful analysis. States are yet another aggregation of roughly this second magnitude, the criteria here being more political and historical. Although there are many thousands of "places," there are about 40 agricultural areas, 50 states, and about 180 economic areas in the United States. A third level of aggregation is the so-called "minor" region such as New England, of which there are nine or ten in the country. (Different definitions yield slightly different regions here.) Finally, there is frequent reference to a

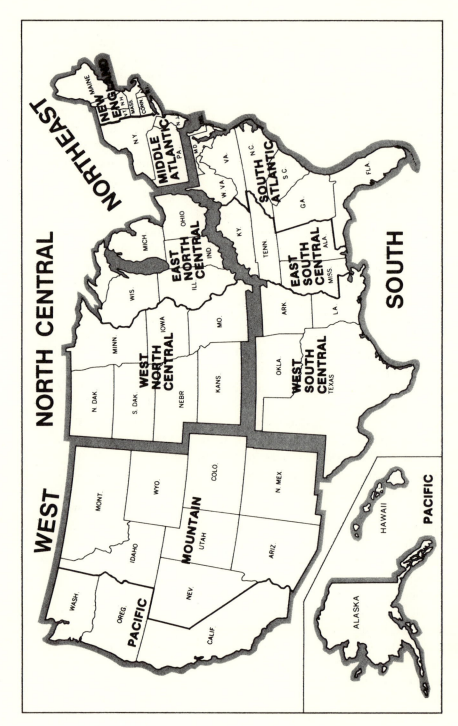

Map 1.1 Regions and Geographic Divisions of the United States. (U.S. Department of Commerce, Bureau of the Census)

highly aggregated set of "major" regions, typically called North-east, North Central, South, and West, or simply North, South, and West.

In this volume we rely heavily on the nine-region division used by the Census Bureau and charted in Map 1.1. This is a reasonable choice for our purposes, but it is not without problems. First of all, two Census regions might well be subdivided. The South Atlantic region ranges from Maryland and Delaware in the north to Florida in the south. The area around Washington—the Wil-mington-Richmond axis—and the more agricultural remainder of the region are, at base, different kinds of places. A similar problem afflicts the geographically huge Mountain region, which is often called part of the "sunbelt" or the "southern tier," even though its northern reaches are stunningly cold. We have not subdivided these regions because doing so would make our analysis difficult to compare with other analyses. Moreover, there is no clear way to subdivide either problematic region. A second problem inher-ent in the nine-region division is that for certain sorts of analysis, special regional classifications are appropriate. The major example of this concerns analysis of agriculture. The country can be divided into units that share soil, temperature, and precipitation patterns, and their agricultural productivity can thus be compared. Analysis of energy or water supplies suggests another division scheme, and analysis of political behavior yet another. Such special classifica-tions do not necessarily match or subdivide Census regions. For our purposes, however, these special divisions are not necessary, and we merely note them here.

Thus far we have emphasized differences among regions, and we will continue to do so throughout the volume. Yet as we suggested above, the regions have some striking similarities, which result from three forces. First, the United States has been influ-enced heavily by internal migration, more so than most modern nations. The original 13 colonies were "settled" by Europeans, who in turn moved west as new territories were opened, pur-chased, or conquered (some purchases and conquests were from other Europeans, of course). Virtually always Americans' families came from somewhere else in or outside the country, the major regional difference being the number of generations between the original migration and the present. This flow from one region to another, which continues and is accelerating today, means that people are more similar across the country than they would be if families evolved *in situ*. Second, the regions of the United States trade heavily with each other. Article I in the United States Constitution makes it illegal for states—and by implication regions—to interfere with this trade. As a result, regional economies influence one another, keeping prices and costs of easily transportable goods more similar than they might be otherwise. In addition, national markets develop, making consumption patterns (and even the appearance of retail establishments) eerily invariant from region to region. Third, it is easy to become familiar with large portions of the United States, either directly (through travel on frequent air flights or extensive, well-built highways) or vicariously (through nationally distributed movies and television programs).

As barriers to migration diminish—as communications and distribution networks improve, for example, or as technology conquers extreme temperatures—the homogeneity of the United States makes it possible for individuals and businesses to move without serious cultural, financial, or social dislocation. The development of cheap window and central air conditioners and the availability of convenient air transportation, for example, had much to do with the sudden attractiveness of Florida to retirees. The forces prompting moves—lifestyle, jobs, housing prices—would be weaker if it were not for these facilitating forces. Even so, these moves are not benign. Massive migration from one region to another has profound effects on both regions, as do mismatches between population and economic shifts. Fundamental regional differences become important, and all this shows up in political activity or further migration. Regional similarity makes these complex flows likely, but the result is regional diversity.

Before we move on to the substantive part of our work, two details require attention: the names we use for different regions and the meaning we give the word *immigration*. The names of the nine Census regions, which appear in Map 1.1, are generally self-explanatory, and we have tried to use them precisely. (We frequently use initials in figures, so East North Central becomes ENC.) But regions have existed longer than this set of names, and thus other regional names arise here and there in the text. "North Central" and "South Central" refer to the obvious two-region combinations. "South" refers to South Atlantic, East South Central, and West South Central. "West" refers to Mountain and Pacific. Finally, "North" refers to New England, Mid-Atlantic,

East North Central, and West North Central. We have tried to
avoid common but ambiguous names like "Plains," "Midwest,"
"Northeast," "Southwest," and the contemporary "sunbelt" and
"frostbelt," but inevitably they appear here and there. In general,
"Northeast" comprises New England and Mid-Atlantic (elsewhere
East North Central is frequently included under this rubric);
"Midwest" and "Plains" are the same as North Central (elsewhere
"Midwest" sometimes refers only to West North Central or to this
plus Wisconsin and Illinois); and "Southwest" means the states
of California, Nevada, Utah, Arizona, Colorado, New Mexico, and
sometimes Texas.

Demographers distinguish three sorts of regional migrants:
those who arrive from another region of the same country, those
who arrive from another country, and those who leave the region.
These groups are often called "*in*migrants," "*im*migrants," and
"*out*migrants," respectively. The important distinction this usage
permits—between inmigrants and immigrants—is less important
in this book than the distinction between those who come into
a region and those who leave it. For this reason we adopt a slightly
different convention. "Immigrants," in this book, are individuals
who move into a given region from elsewhere. When necessary,
we distinguish those who arrive from abroad by calling them
"foreign immigrants." "Emigrants"—the common English antonym for immigrants—refers to individuals who leave a region.
"Net migration," the difference between these two movements
for a region, can be either "net emigration," when there are more
emigrants than immigrants, or "net immigration," when the reverse is true. These distinctions are particularly important for our
demographic discussions in Chapters 2 and 3, but they also apply
to interregional job shifts in Chapter 4.

We conclude from our analysis that the general patterns of
regional divergence that characterized the 1970s will continue
through the 1980s. In general, the South and West will grow
quickly (both economically and demographically), and the North
will grow only slowly. Within these general trends we identify
two subtrends of some importance: the special status within the
North of the New England and West North Central regions (we
project resurging growth for these two regions); and the status
within the South and West of the Pacific and South Atlantic regions
(we project decelerating growth for these two regions). These
projections depart in two respects from most official ones: The

East North Central, and West North Central. We have tried to avoid common but ambiguous names like "Plains," "Midwest," "Northeast," "Southwest," and the contemporary "sunbelt" and "frostbelt," but inevitably they appear here and there. In general, "Northeast" comprises New England and Mid-Atlantic (elsewhere East North Central is frequently included under this rubric); "Midwest" and "Plains" are the same as North Central (elsewhere "Midwest" sometimes refers only to West North Central or to this plus Wisconsin and Illinois); and "Southwest" means the states of California, Nevada, Utah, Arizona, Colorado, New Mexico, and sometimes Texas.

Demographers distinguish three sorts of regional migrants: those who arrive from another region of the same country, those who arrive from another country, and those who leave the region. These groups are often called "*in*migrants," "*im*migrants," and "*out*migrants," respectively. The important distinction this usage permits—between inmigrants and immigrants—is less important in this book than the distinction between those who come into a region and those who leave it. For this reason we adopt a slightly different convention. "Immigrants," in this book, are individuals who move into a given region from elsewhere. When necessary, we distinguish those who arrive from abroad by calling them "foreign immigrants." "Emigrants"—the common English antonym for immigrants—refers to individuals who leave a region. "Net migration," the difference between these two movements for a region, can be either "net emigration," when there are more emigrants than immigrants, or "net immigration," when the reverse is true. These distinctions are particularly important for our demographic discussions in Chapters 2 and 3, but they also apply to interregional job shifts in Chapter 4.

We conclude from our analysis that the general patterns of regional divergence that characterized the 1970s will continue through the 1980s. In general, the South and West will grow quickly (both economically and demographically), and the North will grow only slowly. Within these general trends we identify two subtrends of some importance: the special status within the North of the New England and West North Central regions (we project resurging growth for these two regions); and the status within the South and West of the Pacific and South Atlantic regions (we project decelerating growth for these two regions). These projections depart in two respects from most official ones: The

Chapter 2

REGIONAL GROWTH
IN THE 1980s

Whatever the measure, the regions of the North can expect only minimal growth in the decades to come, while the regions of the South and West can expect substantial growth. Regional projections, which we review briefly in Appendix A, vary considerably; even so, this general consensus is remarkably clear. The first counts of the 1980 Census have confirmed these general predictions dramatically: The population of the United States grew by 23.3 million people during the 1970s, with 89.9 percent of this growth in the five regions of the South and West.

We fully expect this general pattern of growth to continue, in both demographic and economic terms. This general expectation rests on our assessment of the trends that together determine regional growth. In this chapter we discuss our assessment from two perspectives. First, we consider several of the detailed trends that fueled growth through the 1970s. Most of these will continue, in our view, to have profound effects on the demographic, economic, and social structure of regions. Second, we explore the implications of this analysis for each region of the country, an exercise that leads us to make useful distinctions among regions. When regions have exhibited similar aggregate growth patterns in the past, it is tempting to predict that they will grow similarly in the future. Our examination of underlying trends in individual regions suggests some exceptions to this pattern and leads us to predictions that are somewhat different from current projections of regional growth.

Several interrelated trends strike us as particularly important. It is not possible to separate the effects of these trends, but it is possible to organize the discussion around several dominant themes:

1. The extraordinary responsiveness of labor supply to labor demand in some regions, allowing those regions to maintain low wage levels (which attract industry) while increasing employment opportunities and per-capita income (which attract people).
2. The concentration of certain industries in certain regions, which, particularly in conjunction with the relative inefficiency of capital equipment in different regions, distributes slow national economic growth unequally across regions.
3. The continued divergence of regional population growth rates.
4. The ascendancy of migration over natural increase as the most important force shaping population growth patterns of states and regions.
5. The composition of interregional migration, whereby some regions attract young migrants, others attract older migrants, and some attract both.
6. The increasing importance of foreign immigration, both legal and illegal, as a component of overall growth and as a particularly important demographic force in certain regions and in many metropolitan cities.
7. The resurgence of growth in nonmetropolitan areas across the entire United States, which, for the first time in more than 150 years, is causing rural areas and small towns to grow faster, on average, than metropolitan areas.
8. The different fertility patterns in different regions.

We first discuss the economic themes and then turn to regional demographics. (Chapter 3 delves somewhat more deeply into the demographic aspects of regional development, Chapter 4 into its economic aspects.)

Economic Growth

A major feature of recent growth in the United States has been the geographic decentralization of economic activity and population. In aggregate terms, this took the form of a relative shift of employment, income, and population away from the older, more industrialized, densely settled regions of the North toward the "newer" (in terms of maturity of economic structure), less industrialized, and more sparsely settled regions of the South and West. In terms of distribution *within* regions, there has also been a shift of economic activity, away from metropolitan areas to the nonmetropolitan areas of regions.

The second trend, the growth of nonmetropolitan areas, was relatively new in the 1970s and was rather unexpected. It reversed long-standing trends favoring metropolitan growth. Recent changes in the distribution among the large regions, on the other hand, continued longer-standing trends. Only the speed with which they took place in the 1970s was unexpected. The point is that there were two *surprising* characteristics of regional growth in the 1970s, a reversal of some established trends and an acceleration of other trends. The two sets of trends were connected, of course, since much of the growth has been in regions well endowed with nonmetropolitan space.

The Surprises of the 1970s

Long before the 1970s regions exhibited different growth rates of population, employment, and income. For many decades the population, total income, and employment of the poorer and less industrial regions of the nation had been growing more quickly than average, and the reverse was true for the richer, more industrialized regions. The "convergence" extended even to percapita incomes (that is, total personal income divided by total population), which generally rose faster in the poorer regions than in the richer regions. This meant that interregional variation in living standards (levels, not growth rates) was diminishing, because rapid growth in total income in the poorer regions was accompanied by less rapid growth in population.

The booming national economy produced strong growth in total personal income and employment during the 1960s, even in the older, more industrialized regions. Convergence of relative percapita income was fairly rapid during this decade, after having slowed in the 1950s. The major convergent movements in the 1960s were threefold: a sharp decline in the high relative income position of the Pacific region; modest declines in the Mid-Atlantic and East North Central regions; and a sharp increase in the position of the South Atlantic and East South Central region. Two low-income regions, West North Central and West South Central, improved only slightly, while the Mountain region actually declined noticeably and New England remained stable. The South Atlantic's improvement resulted from a large increase in its share of the nation's personal income while its share of population remained stable. The gradual decline in this region's share of U.S. population of the 1940s and 1950s had stopped, but the rise of the 1970s had not yet begun.

It is probably fair to say that in the early 1970s the consensus projection, roughly represented by the 1974 projections of the Bureau of Economic Analysis (BEA) that we include in Appendix A, was that (1) the regional dispersion in growth rates of economic aggregates would narrow, so that the pace of redistribution and decentralization would slacken rather than accelerate; and (2) the dispersion among levels of per-capita income would continue to narrow, thus continuing "convergence" along this dimension. The poorer regions would gain shares of the nation's total personal income faster than shares of its population, and the richer regions would lose shares of personal income faster than shares of population. The first element of the consensus was that the more industrialized North would continue to trail the nation in growth rates of aggregates but by less than it did in the 1960s; the second element was that the less industrialized South and West would continue to lead the nation in growth rates of aggregates but by a smaller margin than in the 1960s. The redistribution of the mass of economic activity from the "more developed" to the "less developed" regions would continue, but at a less rapid pace than before.

By now, with the record of the 1970s in hand, it is obvious that this consensus was a mistake. To avoid repeating this mistake, it is extremely important to understand the reasons it occurred. As it turned out, aggregate growth rates diverged instead of converging; the industrialized states lagged even more badly than had been expected. But this divergence in aggregate growth rates actually contributed greatly to a faster-than-expected convergence in the levels of per-capita income. The growth of income in the South and West, more rapid than expected, helped increase the population, both by attracting new immigrants (from other regions) and by reducing emigration of job seekers. Nonetheless, population growth lagged behind income growth in these regions, so that per-capita income rose. The growth of personal income in the North, even slower than expected, was not matched by net emigration sufficient to keep per-capita income from falling relative to the U.S. average.

Growth in the 1980s and Beyond

The critical question now, in the early 1980s, is not whether the trends of the 1980s and 1990s will be exact extrapolations of the past. They almost certainly will be extrapolations at some level, so we can assume quite safely that redistribution and decentralization will continue. But more detail is needed. At what pace will they continue? Will the divergence of growth rates in the aggregates—total income, population, and employment—continue in the 1980s? If so, the acceleration of the redistribution of the 1970s will continue. Or will the divergence of the 1970s be reversed and the growth rates of aggregates move closer to each other, thus slowing down the pace of redistribution of activity?

In either event, our projections are that convergence in levels of per-capita income, and therefore of living standards, will continue. So long as poor regions grow more quickly than the nation, and so long as the growth in their total income outstrips the growth in their population, the convergence in per-capita income will continue. In other words, convergence of per-capita income is likely to occur whether the growth rates of total income diverge or not. But the speed of per-capita convergence will be greater if there is divergence among growth rates of aggregate personal income: We feel that the faster total income grows in the poorer regions, the more population is likely to lag behind income, and therefore the faster per-capita income will grow.

Income and population do not vary independently, of course; neither, in these times, is it always possible for one region to grow without expense to any other. We turn, therefore, to a schematic description of the economic forces that propel regional growth, and more specifically to the variation in these forces that leads one region to develop a different rate from others or from the nation as a whole. We concentrate on six variables: labor demand, labor supply, population, labor-force participation, investment, and wages.

Labor demand increases in a region when local demand for goods and services increases or when national (or international) demand for goods and services is met by production in that region.

Obviously the latter "export" demand does not apply to non-transportable products such as many services. Local demand for goods and services depends in large part on population size, with standard of living (or per-capita income) playing a secondary role. That is, much local production is intended for individual consumers, whose numbers and affluence are thus important determinants of demand for local products and services. When the population in a region increases, demand for goods and services and therefore labor also increases. (The specific goods and services demanded depend on the age structure of the population, a point we address in Chapter 5.) When firms increase regional production to satisfy national rather than regional demand for products, demand for labor also increases. Regional demand for labor thus depends on two forces: regional population and regional investment to supply national (or in any case extraregional) markets.

Changes in regional *population* are determined by three components, the last two somewhat indistinguishable in practice: fertility, autonomous migration, and endogenous migration. Autonomous migration occurs without regard for the attractiveness of labor markets in the sending or receiving regions; the major example is the migration of retirees to warm, affordable communities. Endogenous migration is migration of individuals who are moving to find or improve their jobs. The distinction is important because it influences the relationship between the demand for labor in a region, which increases with population, and the supply of labor, which increases only with the population of workers.

Regional *investment*, in turn, depends partly on population and partly on production costs. Services, retailing, and other localized businesses must operate close to their markets, and thus their production in a region is closely related to population and personal income. Transportable goods, on the other hand, either can be produced near their markets or can be produced elsewhere and shipped. Some production decisions are geologically or geographically determined. Coal, for example, is produced in certain regions not because coal miners' wages are low or demand for coal is high in those regions but because the coal is there. Similar factors concentrate wheat production in the Plains states, orange growing in Florida and California, and shipbuilding in seaboard states (or those with navigable rivers). When there are no strong geographic reasons to produce goods in a particular region, companies generally respond to increased demand by investing in

regions whose production costs, particularly labor costs, are lowest. *Wages*, the major determinants of labor costs, are low when
the demand for labor is small relative to the supply; they are high
when the reverse is true or, according to some analysts, when
unions keep them high.

Clearly the connection among the forces we have described
thus far is labor supply. *Labor supply* increases when a new
worker moves into a region, when the population of potential
workers in a region grows, or when the percentage of potential
workers who actually seek work increases. New workers are attracted to a region, we argued above, either by the availability
of jobs or by the attractiveness of the housing, food, recreation,
and so on wages can buy. However, individuals make decisions
on the basis of imperfect information. Thus it may not be wages,
specific jobs, or lifestyles that attract workers to certain regions
but rather a more general sense that life is better in the attractive
regions. Living standards influence such judgments heavily. Per-
capita income in a region—or, to be more accurate, the joint effect
of wage levels and the expected *labor-force participation* of family
members, retirees, college-age youth, and so on—is an important
force in interregional shifts of workers and their families; the
perceived cost of living is another.

Under what circumstances, then, can we expect regions to grow
steadily at the expense of other regions, and under what circumstances should we expect such growth to be self-limiting? At a
simple level one might argue that the production of transportable
goods or services (that is, production without specific regional ties)
is most efficient in regions where costs, particularly labor costs,
are lowest; that companies therefore increase production in these
regions; that this increased production increases the demand for
labor in those regions; that the increased demand for labor eventually exhausts the ordinary labor supply in those regions; and
that, as a result of competition for scarce labor, wages rise, moving
the region out of its advantageous position and causing companies
to select another region for their next investment. In the simple
argument, workers do not move from high-wage to low-wage regions, so migration does not abate these trends.

It is clear from the record of the 1960s and 1970s that this
model is too simplistic. Three specific revisions are necessary.
First and perhaps most important, workers (and in this group we
include young adults seeking first jobs) *do* move from high-wage

to low-wage regions, either because they feel that the resulting standard of living is better (perhaps because costs are low, or perhaps because spouses are more likely to find work) or because they fear unemployment in the high-wage region. Second, some regions have extraordinarily elastic labor supplies. This means that there are many "potential" workers who enter the labor force only when there is a strong demand for labor. These potential workers may be women whose children are in school, the families of job-seeking migrants from other regions, casual college students, or simply individuals who work when they know jobs are available but do not even seek work otherwise. Third, the forces limiting regional economic growth are not *simply* wage rates. They are untapped labor supply; housing prices, transportation costs, tax rates, and other influences on living costs; and certain resource limits, such as water and energy supplies.

From this revised perspective, the events of the 1960s and 1970s make better sense. Substantial autonomous migration from the frostbelt to the sunbelt increased population in the latter regions but increased the labor supply more slowly, since many of the migrants were retirees. According to the simple argument, this should have caused labor demand to grow faster than supply, wages to rise, transportable-goods production to locate elsewhere, and endogenous emigration to follow these departing jobs and therefore offset the original autonomous immigration in the receiving regions. However, labor-force participation was relatively low in the sunbelt, and when the demand for labor increased, so did labor-force participation and therefore labor supply. Except for the Pacific, these were low-wage regions, keeping business investment in these regions high and stimulating labor demand still more. The predicted rise in wages (in response to increased demand) did not occur, however, because the high elasticity of the labor supply kept wages low. At the same time, since more individuals were working, per-capita incomes rose: The average individual in these regions had higher income than he or she had before the increase in labor demand. Thus the unconventional result was that the economic attractiveness of these regions to workers *increased*, attracting endogenous immigration in addition to autonomous immigration, *without* the predicted decline in these regions' attractiveness to industrial investment. Where the simple economic argument predicted negative feedback and therefore a convergence of regional growth rates, there was essentially positive feedback and a continued dispersion of regional growth rates.

From the revised perspective on these forces, there is considerable likelihood that regional growth rates will remain dispersed for at least some time. Unless autonomous migration or the responsiveness of endogenous migration to employment and income opportunities diminishes or unless wages in low-wage regions rise, marginal investment in industries or services will flow to the fast-growing regions. As we show in Chapter 4, wage-rate differences have proved remarkably consistent over time, in some cases because of the labor-supply elasticity discussed above and in some cases because of union activity or similar forces. We thus think it likely that demographic shifts, whether autonomous or endogenous, will continue to influence regional growth differences strongly. We devote considerable attention to these differences below. Before we turn to demographic trends, however, one further point requires discussion: the regional distribution of slow growth in the national economy.

The Effects of National Growth

Clearly one reason the projections for the 1970s proved so inaccurate was their implicit (and often explicit) assumption that economic and demographic growth rates would converge quickly—an assumption that, from the perspective outlined above, was premature. There is another reason for the inaccuracy of the projections, specifically the assumption that there would be close to "full employment" in the 1970s. For example, the BEA 1974 exercise we review in Appendix A assumed an unemployment rate of 4 percent. It would have been hard to imagine official projections assuming anything *but* relatively full employment at the time the BEA 1974 projections were made. To have done otherwise would have been to project what was then considered a failure of the federal government's policies. (This problem is of course shared by all official projection agencies and federal administrations.) Moreover, in 1974 the energy-price revolution had not yet come, and the chronic slack needed to moderate inflation was not yet recognized as a fact of life. Indeed, there was little attention paid to the sensitivity of the results to the full-employment assumption. Although it is possible to conceive of "official" projections that tolerate growth-rate divergence, it is hard to imagine that the authors of "official" projections could assume significant "unemployment" (over 5 percent, say) in the future.

In any case, the economy did not approach the low level of unemployment the projectors assumed. On both theoretical and empirical grounds, we would expect such a shortfall in the national growth rate to be spread unevenly across regions, depressing growth in the North more than in the South and West. Thus we would expect slack in the national economy to prevent the narrowing of aggregate growth rates projected for the early 1970s. It might even cause a divergence of growth rates, quite contrary to the consensus projection. Indeed, the contrast between the 1970s and the 1950s—the latter also a slow-growth decade—should have suggested to forecasters how sensitive the North is to slow national growth. We must briefly consider the grounds for expecting this result—for recognizing what actually happened in the 1970s as consistent with although not wholly caused by the national shortfall.

In a sluggish national economy the composition of output differs from that of a full-employment economy: The production of producer durables, consumer durables, and business construction is less than when the economy is at fuller utilization of capacity. The BEA projection methodology explicitly recognizes this, and the article reporting the 1980 projection's results comments on the implications for the North of fuller utilization in the 1980s and 1990s than in the 1970s. On the other hand, consumer nondurables, services, and government nondefense spending are less likely to diminish, at least in the kind of prolonged but generally mild recession the nation suffered in the 1970s.

What if all regions devoted the same share of economic activity to a given industry? If that industry grew or diminished at the same rate in each region, the effects of the national growth or shrinkage would be the same in all regions. This is rarely so for two reasons: Many industries concentrate in certain regions, and growth or shrinkage rates in a given industry often vary from region to region. If one region devotes a larger share of its economy to a given industry than another region, then national growth or shrinkage in that industry will affect the two regions differently, even if the industry grows or shrinks in each region at the national rate. For example, the manufacture of consumer durables is disproportionately prominent in the economy of the East North Central region. If consumer durables grow at the same below-average rate in all regions, then, even though consumer durables grow at the same (slow) rate in the South Atlantic and East North Central regions, the effect of this slow growth is greater in the latter. In the extreme, if an industry is entirely located within a particular subset of regions (as, for example, oil and gas production is), and that industry grows at a rate different from that of other industries, then the only regions to benefit or suffer are those where that industry is active. The industries that grew relatively slowly because of the low-employment economy during the 1970s—durables manufacturing and business construction—are indeed concentrated in certain regions, and thus slow growth hurt these regions, the northern ones, more than others.

Complicating matters still further, it is not generally true that an industry that is shrinking nationally—as some did in the 1970s—shrinks at the same rate in each region where it is active. Instead, shrinking industries generally optimize their operations by decreasing activity more quickly wherever production facilities are least efficient. This generally means that older capacity is idled first. In most multiregional industries, the older, less efficient plants are located in the North. When the production of consumer durables declined nationally, it declined even faster in these regions. Since these regions were also those heavily invested in consumer durables, the effects of concentration and of optimization compounded each other. (The resulting shifts in mix are outlined in Chapter 4.) In technologically evolving industries the latter effect is sometimes irreversible. Older plants do not reopen when demand revives, since the financial difference between reopening an older, "temporarily" closed plant (which usually involves re-tooling) and expanding a newer, more efficient one is often small. Moreover, when the newer, more efficient plant is in a low-wage region, then even if reopening and expansion costs are equivalent, it may be less expensive at the margin to expand the newer (and generally southern) plant rather than reopen the closed (and generally northern) one. Only when expansion costs sufficiently exceed reopening costs—as, for example, when land or construction costs are high—does the situation reverse, and even then the reversal takes effect only when the industry begins to grow once more.

Our reassessment of regional growth in the 1970s suggests that the unexpectedly steady divergence in aggregate growth rates (and the consequent convergence of per-capita incomes, or standards

of living) stemmed not from an aberrant set of economic circumstances but rather from the continuing effects of basic economic
and demographic forces. Much economic growth is directly related
to demographic growth, and vice versa. Our analysis suggests that
this circular effect works to the benefit of certain regions because
these regions combine the ability to draw autonomous migration,
historically low wage rates, and a labor supply elastic enough to
prevent economic growth from driving up wages. Other regions
lose population and industrial activity (relatively, if not absolutely)
because personal income shares shrink faster than population
shares (or rise more slowly than population), thus reducing per-
capita income and standard of living; because they are unable to
retain or attract autonomous migrants; because the labor supply
is inelastic, making industrial expansion self-limiting; or because
their production costs—as determined by wages and the efficiency
of existing plants—are high.

These forces account for most regional divergence in the 1970s.
We do not see that any of them has been mitigated in any substantial way, so we expect continued regional divergence into the
1980s. We will consider three possible exceptions to this prediction further on: the Pacific region, which thus far has exhibited
strong growth, despite high prices and high wages; the South
Atlantic region, whose labor supply seems to be losing its elasticity, thus driving up wages and inhibiting new investment; and
the West North Central region, whose rural areas may increasingly
hold residents who might in earlier decades have migrated to the
urban South (or reattract those who did so). First, however, we
turn to projections of population growth.

Population Growth

The revised model relating population, labor-market, and economic trends suggests that the flows of migrants in the 1970s,
primarily from the North to the West and South, correspond
closely to emerging economic differences among the regions.
These economic differences, which allowed per-capita incomes to
grow independently of wages in some regions, are unlikely to
disappear quickly. Thus, from our perspective it seems likely that
the trends of the 1970s will continue for some time. The Census
Bureau's projections of regional population growth generally rest

on assumptions that regional differences along certain basic dimensions of population growth—such as migration and fertility—will attenuate over time, and thus the "official" expectation has been that the demographic divergence of the 1970s will slow in decades to come.

The first counts of the 1980 Census have confirmed what some demographers had suspected for several years. Instead of being an aberration, the decade of the 1970s ushered in a new dynamic for population growth that is having and will continue to have a profound effect on the demographic, economic, and social structure of American society. Five elements of this dynamic stand out: divergence in regional growth rates; ascendancy of net migration over natural increase as a determinant of these; dramatic change in age structures across the nation; growth in nonmetropolitan areas; and increasingly important foreign immigration.

We focus, in this section of Chapter 2, on the first three of these trends, attending particularly to the differences between projected and actual population in 1980 and to the implications of these differences for 1990 projections. Our own projections of future growth, which emerge from analysis of these differences, differ in several respects from the Census projections of 1990 regional population. Chapter 3 analyzes the population trends of the last two decades in considerably more detail and provides more discussion of our projections. Before we turn to our present discussion of growth rates, migration, and age structures, however, the other two trends we mentioned above require brief comment (each is discussed further in Chapter 3).

For most of the nation's history, metropolitan areas have grown faster than nonmetropolitan areas, at first because the former were so small and later because the industrial structure of the society came to favor concentrated (and therefore urban) growth. In the 1970s, for the first time in 150 years, rural areas and small towns grew faster than urban areas—a trend that has been attributed variously to the virtual completion of the Interstate highway system, the cost of urban housing, the changing lifestyle of the typical American, and the definition of *urban*. Whatever its cause, the resurgence of nonmetropolitan growth affects regions differently or—perhaps—is a result of differences among regions' growth patterns.

Foreign immigration led to the founding of the United States, and over the nation's history further waves of immigration have had major effects on the population. Foreign immigration has never distributed itself evenly across the regions. It is no surprise, for example, that immigrants to northern states more frequently come from Europe, that immigrants to southeastern states come from Caribbean islands or Africa, and that immigrants to southwestern states generally come from Asia or Latin America. Nor is it any surprise that relatively few foreign immigrants now end up in West North Central states. During the 1970s patterns of foreign immigration once again had a substantial impact, as large numbers of Asian and Latin American immigrants entered the Pacific and Mountain regions, and foreign immigration to other regions (from whatever source) failed to keep pace. The recent influx of Cuban refugees into the South Atlantic region has changed this somewhat, but it can do so no more than temporarily. A second dimension of this shift in foreign immigration complicates analysis significantly: The increasing percentage that is undocumented—in either the legal or the demographic sense.

The new growth dynamic has caused official population projections and (as we show in Appendix A) many economic forecasts built upon such projections to be problematic as tools for planning and policy making. We have ventured some judgments about likely demographic trends through 1990. The resulting numbers, we must say at the outset, are not projections in the technical sense, whereby a formal model emits exact numbers under a wide range of various well-defined assumptions. There is little point to building such a model before the detailed 1980 Census data provide a good jump-off point for the projections. Our considerably less formal projections are based on a careful consideration of recent aggregate trends and on an evaluation of differences between projections of the 1980 population based on the trends of the early and mid-1970s and the actual population counted in 1980. We attempt to formulate and justify assumptions about future trends that make sense for the decade of the 1980s. Our projections of population growth thus can be considered as "targets" consistent with realistic future trends in the two components of growth, natural increase (births less deaths) and net migration (immigrants less emigrants).

Our approach, to be sure, is different from the projection methodology used by the Census Bureau. Census projections employ a set of often arbitrary assumptions, such as convergence of state and regional trends toward the national average, and consider demographic trends to be independent of any regional economic trends unless those economic trends are reflected in demographic history. This approach is often justified as necessary to produce long-range projections (to the year 2050, say), but the corollary of this argument is that the projections' intermediate estimates of births, deaths, and migration statistics are insensitive to current trends and highly inaccurate in the short term of a decade or less.

We begin our discussion of expected trends in regional population growth by contrasting Census Bureau projections with our own projections of net growth through the 1980s. The Census Bureau projections are based on what might be called a "hypo-thetical" scenario. The Series II-B projections incorporate the following hypothetical trends: (1) Present differences in fertility among the states and regions converge to a national average set of age-specific birth rates consistent with 2.1 births per woman (Series I and III call for 1.7 and 2.7 births, respectively) by the year 2020; and (2) migration rates hold constant at the levels estimated for the period 1970–1975 (Series A assumes 1965–1975 migration trends). It is important to point out that the Census Bureau makes no claim that these hypothetical trends are likely to occur but, rather, calls the projections "illustrative." Users of the projections, however, typically pick Series II-B as the "most likely" scenario and use these projections as forecasts when future population counts are needed for planning or policy analysis.

Likely Growth Trends

Over the decade of the 1980s actual population growth in states and regions should deviate substantially from Census Bureau projections. Table 2.1 and Figure 2.1 present comparable Joint Center and Census projections to 1990. (Table 2.2 presents the historical population data plotted in Figure 2.1.) The 1990 populations of the New England, Mid-Atlantic, East North Central, and South Atlantic regions are larger according to the Census projections than they are according to our projections. The reverse is true elsewhere. These differences tend to balance each other, so the Census projections for the total population of the United States in 1990 deviate from the total 1990 Joint Center projections by only about 2 percent. However, differences between Joint Center

**Table 2.1   Population Projections to 1990: Census Series II-B and Joint
Center Forecasts (population in thousands)**

Region	1990 Census II-B	1990 Joint Center
New England	13,600	13,250 (± 2.5%)
East North Central	43,260	41,500 (± 2.5%)
West North Central	18,101	19,000 (± 2.5%)
Mid-Atlantic	38,196	34,000 (± 2.5%)
South Atlantic	42,727	40,500 (± 2.5%)
East South Central	15,526	18,250 (± 2.5%)
West South Central	25,254	29,750 (± 4.0%)
Mountain	12,936	15,000 (± 5.0%)
Pacific	33,405	37,000 (± 3.5%)
Total U.S.	243,005	248,250 (± 2.0%)

projections and Census projections at the regional level are substantial, ranging from 2.6 percent in New England to 15 percent
in the two South Central regions.

We attach to most of our regional population projections a potential error of 2.5 percent either way. In three regions—West
South Central, Mountain, and Pacific—greater uncertainty about
underlying trends leads us to be slightly more cautious in estimating potential error. Because the difference between our projection and the Census projection for 1990 is less than twice our
estimate of potential error in only two cases, we are confident that
the pattern of differences we predict does reflect the difference
between our reliance on recent data and convergence assumptions.
It is likely that by 1990 there will be about 8.5 million fewer
people living in the four northern regions and about 14 million
more living in the five southern and western regions than the
Census II-B projections suggest.

We project lower fertility and more net emigration in three
northern regions than Census does. During the decade of the
1980s, the Mid-Atlantic region should continue to lose population,
with both New Jersey and Pennsylvania joining New York as
shrinking states. Likewise, Massachusetts and Connecticut are
strong candidates to lose population because their low birth rates
are insufficient to offset the net emigration and death rates they
will experience. But large expected gains in the population of the
three northern New England states will keep the region's population growing, if only slightly. In contrast, no East North Central

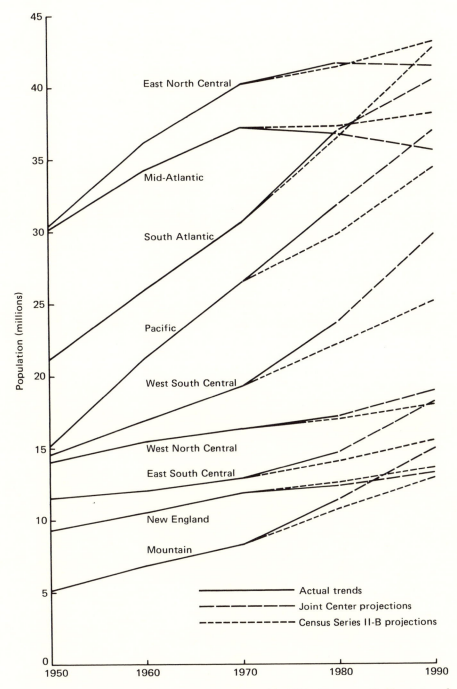

Figure 2.1 Population by Census Region, 1950–1990. (*Sources: Tables 2.1 and 2.2*)

Table 2.2 Population of U.S. Census Regions, 1950–1980

Census Region	Population (thousands)				Rate of Growth over Decade (%)		
	1950	1960	1970	1980	1950–1960	1960–1970	1970–1980
Total U.S.	151,375	179,322	203,296	226,502	18.5	13.4	11.4
New England (ME, NH, VT, MA, RI, CT)	9,315	10,509	11,848	12,349	12.8	12.7	4.2
East North Central (OH, IN, IL, MI, WI)	30,400	36,224	40,262	41,668	19.2	11.1	3.5
West North Central (MN, IA, MO, ND, SD, NE, KS)	14,062	15,395	16,323	17,183	9.5	6.0	5.3
Mid-Atlantic (NY, NJ, PA)	30,163	34,168	37,209	36,788	13.2	8.9	−1.1
South Atlantic (DE, MD, DC, VA, WV, NC, SC, GA, FL)	21,183	25,972	30,678	36,942	22.6	18.1	20.4
East South Central (KY, TN, AL, MS)	11,478	12,050	12,808	14,663	4.9	6.3	14.5
West South Central (AR, LA, OK, TX)	14,583	16,951	19,326	23,743	16.2	14.0	22.9
Mountain (MT, ID, WY, CO, NM, AZ, UT, NV)	5,076	6,855	8,289	11,369	35.0	20.9	37.2
Pacific (WA, OR, CA, AK, HI)	15,115	21,198	26,553	31,797	40.2	25.3	19.7

SOURCE: U. S. Census Bureau, *Historical Statistics of the United States: Colonial Times to 1970; Advance Reports*, 1980 Census of Population and Housing.

state will attract enough population to offset losses in the region's other states which are projected to shrink. Although no East North Central state is expected to lose population as rapidly as the three Mid-Atlantic states will, likely losses due to emigration and low fertility in the region's two largest states, Ohio and Illinois, should cause the region as a whole to begin to lose some population by 1990.

The one eastern region that has maintained a high level of growth during the 1970s, South Atlantic, should abruptly reduce its growth rate during the 1980s, mostly because its natural increase will remain low. Florida, the state whose attractiveness to retirees has paced the region in growth for more than three decades, probably will lose its historical share of potential retirees to other states in the East South Central, West South Central, and Mountain states in particular and to nonmetropolitan areas in general. The recent migration of young adults to the South Atlantic states should abate as jobs continue to shift to the balance of the sunbelt and Mountain states, as well as to nonmetropolitan areas throughout the country.

We predict no "surprises" with respect to population growth in the five remaining regions of the country. The regions that grew rapidly during the 1970s are expected to continue to do so during the 1980s, particularly the East South Central, West South Central, and Mountain regions, where high fertility combines with high net immigration. Growth will take place in both metropolitan and nonmetropolitan areas of these regions.

The West North Central region has in the past grown only slowly, with natural increase just offsetting net emigration. The West North Central states should benefit particularly from reduced rural emigration, since historically rural areas have accounted for much of the region's emigration. During the 1980s emigration from the West North Central region should end and perhaps reverse itself, and immigration would thus reinforce natural increase.

The Pacific states should continue to grow at a strong pace throughout the decade, although we have attached a slightly higher level of uncertainty to the 1990 estimate of total population than we have in all but two other regions. This uncertainty stems from the fact that California's attractiveness for immigrants faltered in the early 1970s and revived in the late 1970s, suggesting that California's population growth is particularly sensitive to fluctuations in its and the nation's economic health. Other Pacific states picked up the slack in California's growth during the 1970s. If Washington and Oregon have grown by attracting Californians, our projection of Pacific growth should be smaller than the figures in Table 2.1; if they have attracted immigrants from outside the region, the Pacific region's population will fall on the high side of our estimated growth range. The source of this migration will be known when more of the 1980 Census data are analyzed and published.

The 1980 Census

Regional population totals for 1980 differed from expected totals for two reasons. First, as widely reported, the total United States population proved to be over 227 million people, some 5 million more than the Census Bureau had expected to count. Second, the Census Bureau's estimates of interregional migration and regional fertility were mistaken, compounding the effects of the national underexpectation. These two sources of error caused the errors graphed in Figure 2.1, which vary considerably by region.

What caused the Census Bureau's overall expectations and its findings to be five million people apart? It is tempting to view the unexpected surfeit of U.S. residents as the product of a child-bearing spree, but in fact many of the unexpected residents must have been born in time for the 1970 count. (The reason is partly that so many are over ten years old and partly that intercensal birth data are relatively accurate.) Where, then, were they? We suggest three answers to this question. Some were outside the United States, and the prevalence of undocumented foreign immigration by 1970 caused the overall foreign immigration rate to be underestimated. Others were living in households not properly counted under the 1970 Census methodology, and either they moved into more ordinary households, or the Census methods became more sensitive between 1970 and 1980. And still others lived longer than the Census Bureau expected.

The errors in regional migration and fertility patterns are more complex. We discuss them in the remainder of this section. Note that at the regional level we cannot disentangle the effects of the migration errors from the undercount errors. Figure 2.2 contrasts the actual increase (or decrease) in different age groups in each of the nine census regions for the decade ending in 1980 with the

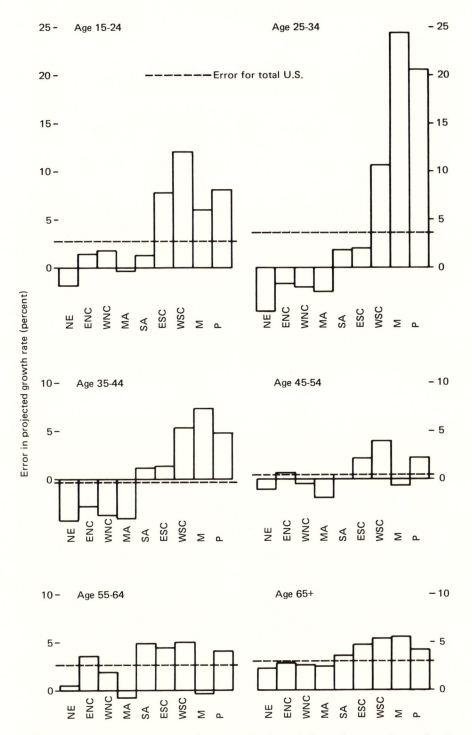

Figure 2.2   Error in Projected 1970–1980 Growth Rates by Age Group for Regions: U.S. Census Projections, Series II-B.

increase (or decrease) that was expected under the Census II-B projections. The errors in the projected growth rates are differences between projected and actual rates of increase for each region. (The base data are in Appendix Table C.1.) We have excluded the population under 15 years of age from this figure because we want to reserve for Chapter 3 our discussion of the complex differences between Census fertility projections and actual trends in births.

The distribution of the five-million-person error across the United States as a whole is marked by the dotted line in each panel of Figure 2.2. Thus, for example, in both the 15–24 and 25–34 age groups, the projected rate of increase for the nation as a whole was more than 2.5 percentage points below the actual rate of growth for those age groups. A substantial part of the "surplus" population growth in the young adult ages certainly is due to foreign immigration, but an important part may comprise unmarried native-born Americans not residing with their parents. Unattached young adults, many of whom constantly change living arrangements, are notoriously difficult for Census to enumerate. The growth of this unattached population between 1970 and 1980 reflected the passage of the baby-boom generation into the young-adult age groups, delays in marriage and higher divorce rates, and the increasing level of independent living among young adults during the 1970s. As this population expanded, its very size made its sometimes odd living arrangements more "legitimate," and there is the distinct possibility that the Census Bureau, which had doubled its efforts to reach groups missed in prior Censuses, enumerated a larger percentage of these individuals in 1980 than in 1970.

Whatever the source of this unexpected proliferation of young adults, it is clear from the first two panels of Figure 2.2 that its growth was not evenly distributed across regions. Where immigration played a large role in population growth over the decade—as we will see in Chapter 3, the West South Central, Mountain, and Pacific regions—growth for the 15–24 age group was 7 to 12 percentage points higher than projected. In these same regions, the 25–34 age group grew at rates that were 12 to 25 percentage points higher than expected from the 1970–1974 migration patterns built into Census II-B projections. The growth in the 15–24 and 25–34 age groups in the North and East, which was less than expected, is also shown in Figure 2.2. The 15–24 age group in

both New England and Mid-Atlantic had less growth than expected, and for the 25–34 age group this also applied to the East
North Central and West North Central regions. The South Atlantic
region, while growing more than expected in the 15–24 and 25–34
age groups, did not account for a proportional share of the unexpected growth in the United States.

The same pattern of higher-than-expected growth in the South
and West and lower-than-expected growth in the North and East
is repeated in the 35–44 age group and, with a few minor exceptions, in the 45–54 age group as well. The levels of error in
the migrant-attracting regions are markedly lower in these two
middle-age groups, and the overall growth for the United States
was fairly close to what the Census Bureau predicted. The exception to the overall growth pattern for the first four age groups
is the 45–54 age group in the Mountain states: Growth was *below*
expected levels during the 1970s.

The last two age groups in Figure 2.2 repeat one attribute of
the first two age groups, namely, higher than expected growth
for the nation as a whole. However, the growth in the 55–64 and
over–65 age groups is more evenly distributed across regions,
indicating that the likely source of the error is people living longer
than was expected. Since retirement and "preretirement" migra-
tions to warmer climates are important elements of overall migration in the United States, the South and West received a
greater share of this unexpected growth. An exception once again
is the Mountain region for the 55–64 age group, which behaved
strangely like the Mid-Atlantic region in growing more slowly than
expected.

Were it not for the unexpected longevity of the older population
in the North, total population growth over the 1970s in these
regions would have been even lower than that observed in Figure
2.1. This important trend, combined with the lower-than-expected
increase of young adults in the same regions, yields a population
in this part of the country that is aging (in the distributional sense)
much more rapidly than expected, a point that will be further
discussed in Chapter 3.

In the aggregate, the Census Bureau was more accurate in
projecting births than in projecting deaths between 1975 and 1980,
coming within 1 percent of births and 4 percent of deaths for the
nation as a whole. The range of error across regions for the births,
however, was greater than the range of error for deaths. Errors

in the Series II birth projections ranged from a 12 percent over-estimate in New England to a 9 percent underestimate in the Mountain region. The range for errors in death projections ranged from an 8 percent overestimate for the Mid-Atlantic to a 1 percent underestimate for the West South Central region. The North and East, which here includes the South Atlantic region, generally had fewer births than Census projected, whereas the rest of the country had more births than projected (see Figure 2.3).

Two factors are responsible for this general pattern of error. First, the northern regions did not move rapidly toward total fertility rates of 2.1 births per woman, as the Series II projections assumed they would. Second, more young adults in the prime childbearing ages moved, on a net basis, from low-fertility into high-fertility regions than the projections assumed, yet the high fertility in the receiving regions did not decline. The one exception to this appears to be the South Atlantic; young migrants here seem to have kept their fertility low. Without further analysis we cannot say whether such migrants move to the high-fertility regions *in order* to start a family sooner or simply find themselves behaving more like the natives when they arrive.

Compared with the 1960s, fertility declined unusually fast during the first half of the 1970s. Such a decline certainly suggests that many young couples either were thwarted in their desires to settle down and start a family or chose not to do so. The higher fertility after 1975 may indicate that postponed family formation was being made up, especially since the states in which the fertility decline bottomed out most quickly and started to rise earliest were the states receiving the largest share of net immigrants between 1975 and 1980.

For the United States as a whole, the Census Bureau mispredicted only one birth or death for each nine mispredicted migrants over the 1975–1980 period. The migration projections made by the Census Bureau are error-laden because the actual migration trends differ markedly from the assumptions about future migration trends that Census builds into its projection model. The decade of the 1970s was a period in which demographic trends renewed their regional divergence after an unusual—but temporary—period of convergence. The projection models, on the other hand, reflect assumptions of convergence (in the case of fertility) or stability (in the case of migration). Such assumptions may be valid for estimating long-term averages—those extending

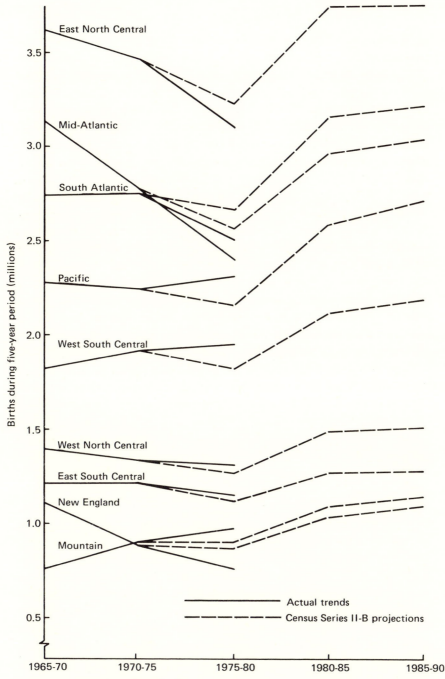

Figure 2.3 **Number of Births by Census Region: U.S. Census Projections, Series II-B.** Estimate of births for 1975–1980 from January 1, 1975 to December 31, 1979; for 1970–1975 from April 1, 1970 to July 1, 1975; for 1965–1970 from January 1, 1965 to December 31, 1969. All other figures from July 1 to June 30.

over many decades—but they do not yield accurate short-term projections.

The unreasonable implications of these convergence and stability assumptions can be seen in Figures 2.4a and 2.4b. The only difference between the two figures is the assumed (stable) level of net migration. Figure 2.4a depicts the Series A projections, which bring all migration rates to 1965–1975 average levels. These projections implied greater homogeneity across regions in migration patterns than did the Series B projections, depicted in Figure 2.4b, which bring migration rates to 1970–1975 averages. The gradual convergence of growth rates in these figures reflects the Series II assumption that fertility will converge to 2.1 births per woman. The discrepancy between the actual trends over the 1970–1980 period and the projected trends based on frozen age-specific migration rates (with the only factor changing the number of migrants being the changing age structure) is apparent in these figures. Practically without exception, regions that actually experienced an increase in their population growth rate had been projected to grow more slowly; those whose growth rates declined between 1970 and 1980 had been projected to grow at an increased pace. This systematic discrepancy arose simply because the projection model called for upward-trending regional migration rates to return to their lower 1965–1975 or 1970–1975 average and for downward-trending regional immigration rates to rise in similar fashion.

Future Trends in Migration and Natural Increase

For most regions, as we have seen, the differences between Census and Joint Center estimates of population growth through the 1980s reflect different assumptions about net migration. In New England, East North Central, and South Atlantic, differences in natural increase are also important. In each case, natural increase will be significantly lower than Census estimates. We expect natural increase to be lower because the cohorts of the baby-boom generation in these regions, who have been "postponing" marriage and fertility in these regions, are not expected to fully "make up" the ground they have lost relative to the same cohorts living in other parts of the country (as is explicitly assumed in the Census projections). The gap between Joint Center and Census assumptions about future natural increase is largest in the South Atlantic region and smallest in the New England states.

In the South Atlantic region, fertility after age 20, over the past decade, has been the lowest of any region in the country. Birth expectation data from this region suggest that low fertility will continue. Low expectations for completed lifetime fertility characterize both white and black women in the South Atlantic region, with black women in their twenties actually expecting fewer lifetime births than white women of the same age. Why this should be true is not well understood, but it could be related to patterns of female labor-force participation and household economics in the South Atlantic region that are particularly demanding of women's time. (We note in Chapter 4, for example, that service employment—and therefore presumably the availability of part-time or flexible service jobs for working mothers—is disproportionately low in this region.) In New England, we expect more convergence toward the Census estimate of natural increase because of the traditionally later ages of childbearing in the Northeast. Increased levels of childbearing are expected from the cohorts of the baby boom as they pass through their mid-twenties in the 1980s. In addition, three New England states (Maine, New Hampshire, and Vermont) are expected to gain population through net migration during the 1980s. Since migrants are typically young adults in the childbearing ages, more New England births will result. Although the Mid-Atlantic region has also experienced higher-than-average fertility among women aged 25 to 30, we expect the economic climate to be less favorable there than in New England. Thus less of total expected fertility will be "made up" in New York, New Jersey, and Pennsylvania. The Mid-Atlantic states should lose potential parents through net emigration during the 1980s, as should the East North Central region.

States in the Northeast are experiencing relatively low fertility, relatively more deaths (because of larger elderly populations), and at best meager migration gains. This pattern and the combination of high fertility, low death rates, and high net immigration in the Southwest and West produce a strong pattern of *divergence* in population growth among the nine regions. The Mountain region has momentum for high growth because of the high sustained levels of fertility throughout the reproductive ages characteristic of this region. High net immigration of young adults into the

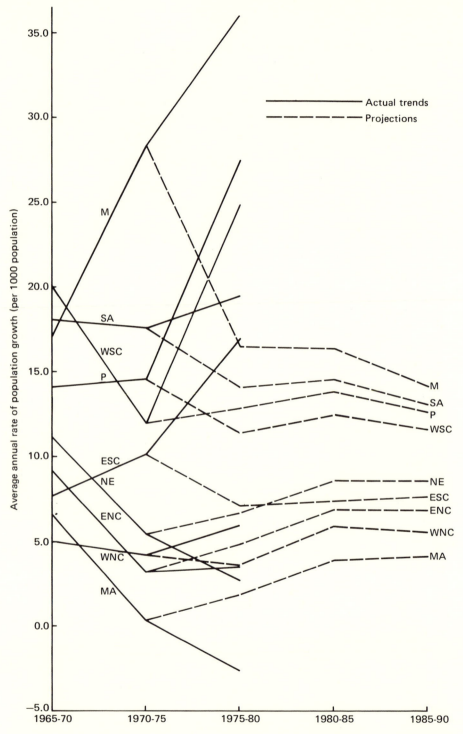

Figure 2.4(a) **U.S. Census Projections of Regional Growth Rates (per 1,000 population): Series II-A.** Total fertility rate 2.1; Migration at 1965–1975 levels.

38

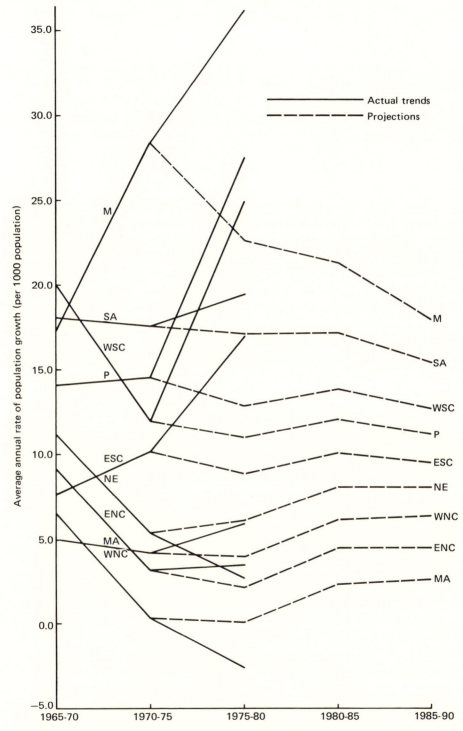

35.0

30.0 ———— Actual trends
- - - - - Projections

25.0

M

20.0

SA

WSC

15.0
P

ESC
10.0
NE

ENC

5.0
MA
WNC

0.0

−5.0

Average annual rate of population growth (per 1000 population)

M

SA

WSC

P

ESC

NE

WNC

ENC

MA

1965-70   1970-75   1975-80   1980-85   1985-90

Figure 2.4(b)   U.S. Census Projections of Regional Growth Rates (per 1,000 population): Series II-B. Total fertility rate 2.1; Migration at 1970–1975 levels.

39

Mountain region will be translated into high levels of natural increase in the 1990s. To a lesser degree, this is true for the Pacific region as well. The East South Central region has very high levels of fertility among women in their teens and early twenties but shares with its South Atlantic neighbor below-average fertility among women in their late twenties and thirties. This all suggests that South Atlantic and East South Central natural increase will be substantially lower than the Mountain natural increase.

The West South Central region, having attracted a large number of young adult migrants during the 1970s, is also expected to have substantial growth due to natural increase. As in the East South Central region, however, natural increase will be attenuated by women's sharply curtailed fertility in the later childbearing ages. If women in the West South Central region begin to adopt a fertility pattern similar to that of their Mountain or Pacific counterparts, natural increase could be even higher and push expected growth above the 25 percent we estimate for the 1990s.

The net migration trends of the 1970s are expected to continue into the 1980s, except for the South Atlantic and perhaps the West North Central region. We expect less growth in the South Atlantic for two reasons. First, other regions of the country should draw off some of the retiree migrants that traditionally have gone to the South Atlantic region in search of a lower cost of living and a more congenial climate. Second, the region has limited potential for nonmetropolitan population growth. The 20 percent growth experienced over each of the past three decades in the South Atlantic region should be cut in half during the 1980s. The attraction of nonmetropolitan areas should reduce migration into the Mountain and Pacific regions as well. (The Mountain region, although well endowed with open space, has relatively little land appropriate or available for population or development.) Some emigrants who leave the older metropolitan areas in the frostbelt in search of a better life will forsake the younger metropolitan alternatives in Los Angeles, San Jose, San Francisco, Denver, Houston, and Tucson in favor of small towns and rural areas in the New England, East South Central, and West North Central regions. We have forecast slightly accelerated rate growth in these last-mentioned regions—implying a modest reversal for West North Central—as small towns and rural areas hold on to their own young people and perhaps attract back those who left for metropolitan areas in the three decades following World War II.

Regional Growth

In the first two sections of this chapter, we considered several trends that underlie regional growth, trends suggesting to us that the divergent growth patterns that have characterized regions for the past two decades will continue into the next. In this we disagree with most official projections of regional growth, which generally assume that the basic tendency of regional growth rates is to converge. In this section we review our projections of regional growth, this time focusing on one region at a time instead of one economic or demographic trend at a time. The nine census regions align themselves into four groups, and it is thus we will discuss them: the fast-growth East South Central, West South Central, and Mountain regions; the no-growth Mid-Atlantic and East North Central regions; the decelerating Pacific and South Atlantic regions; and the resurgent New England and West North Central regions.

Fast-Growth Regions

The first section of this chapter outlined the basis for fast growth in a region: low wages, low labor-force participation, and attractive lifestyle. We can caricature the resulting process as follows: Autonomous migration increases population, this increases labor demand, this increases labor-force participation, this increases per-capita income, and this increases endogenous migration; at the same time wages remain relatively low, thus attracting marginal investment in new (or expanded) production facilities. Although this scenario is an oversimplification, it seems to be a helpful one. As Chapter 4 shows, these were the conditions in the East South Central, West South Central, and Mountain regions in the 1960s, and growth in these regions has followed the predicted path. Wages have not in fact remained constant, since the demand for labor has somewhat outstripped the supply, but nevertheless they are the lowest in the nation and are expected to stay so. As Chapter 4 shows, per-capita incomes in these regions have approached the national average far more quickly than have hourly wages or annual earnings per employee.

The share of these regions' economies devoted to manufacturing has risen over the past two decades, but even so, it is low. As a result, these regions are less sensitive to recessions in manufacturing than more industrialized regions are; moreover, since the manufacturing plant in these regions is relatively new and efficient, it is, in general, the last to be idled. There are forces other than recession or labor shortage that can limit economic growth, but most of them—energy prices, transportation bottlenecks, high taxes, and so on—are more favorable in the fast-growing regions than elsewhere.

One striking difference among the fast-growth regions is in their age-specific fertility patterns. As we show in Chapter 3, women in the southern states, including the two South Central regions, tend to have children relatively early, often completing their families by age 25. Women in the Mountain states, on the other hand, tend to have above-average fertility throughout the reproductive ages. This means that population growth due to natural increase will be steeper but shorter in the two South Central regions than it will be in the Mountain region—unless, as suggested above, prospective Mountain parents begin to behave like Southerners, or vice versa.

Migration into the fast-growth regions consists both of autonomous migrants, primarily retirees, and of endogenous migrants attracted by rising per-capita incomes and low unemployment. As we indicated in the preceding section, there is limited evidence from the 1980 Census that older individuals are leaving the Mountain region in larger numbers than had been expected, perhaps because urban growth in that region has been extremely rapid, and nonretirement, nonmetropolitan options for adults over 45 are more attractive in other regions. (One hypothesis—that this shift represents West North Central emigrants returning home after their time in the sun—is attractive and consistent with the pattern in that region, but it is also unverifiable.)

We thus see both economic and demographic growth in these regions through the 1980s, the former fueled by low wages and an elastic labor supply and the latter by attractive climates and increasing per-capita incomes. It does not hurt, of course, that a major "natural" industry in these regions, energy-related mining, is doing extremely well.

No-Growth Regions

The heavily industrialized states in the Mid-Atlantic and East North Central regions have stopped growing along several dimensions, and several have lost population or employment in specific industries. This is likely to continue. These regions have never attracted enough autonomous migrants to offset their emigration losses of retirees, and as industry and employment have grown in the southern regions, these northern regions have stopped attracting net endogenous migration as well. Labor-force participation in these regions generally has been high, making the labor supply inelastic and causing wages to rise with increases in labor demand. Unionization has also been high in these regions. It is widely argued that when industrial activity shrinks, as it does in a recession, unions act to maintain wage levels rather than employment levels. Unless the idled northern plant can be restarted without retooling or other capital improvements, this "sticky-wage" phenomenon can make it expensive for industries to restore production in the no-growth regions when the business cycle reverses. Instead, they expand production in the fast-growing low-wage regions. As a result, there has been—and is likely to be—little industrial growth in the Mid-Atlantic and East North Central regions.

The demographics of these regions reinforce this prediction. Although much emigration from the no-growth regions comprises retirees, a substantial portion involves individuals or families of childbearing age. The potential parents who remain in these regions do not make up for the emigrants; instead, they have fewer children than their counterparts in other regions, and they have them later. The result is slow (and for an increasing number of states negative) population growth, which causes local industries to slow in the region along with national industries. If household structures did not change, this combination of rather bleak trends might eventually depress housing prices enough to attract (or keep) autonomous migrants and to have some favorable retention effects on endogenous migrants as well. Instead, household sizes are shrinking, and therefore the number of households is rising in these regions, as it is across the country.

Decelerating Regions

Although we group the Pacific and South Atlantic regions under this rubric, they are in fact quite dissimilar. During the 1940s and 1950s—and indeed, for some time before that—the South Atlantic region was largely poor and agricultural, and it lost young people to more industrial regions with some regularity. This population loss stopped during the 1960s as the South industrialized and Florida began to attract retirees. It became population gain as young adults stayed (or returned) to work in the region's new industries during the following decade. The Pacific region, on the other hand, has grown steadily since the transcontinental railroads were completed in the last few decades of the nineteenth century. The Pacific region's wages are high; the South Atlantic's are low. Why, then, do we group them here?

Growth in the South Atlantic region is, we believe, reaching limits. The major signs of this are the rapidly declining birth rate noted above, diminished total-fertility expectations, and a reduced share of migrating retirees, all of which in combination promise to slow population growth dramatically. At the same time labor-force participation has risen in the South Atlantic, and thus further increases in labor-force participation are less able to offset reduced population growth. If industrial growth continues under these circumstances, labor demand will rise more quickly than labor supply; the supply will prove inelastic; wages will rise (as they have been doing); and industry will invest elsewhere, presumably in the fast-growth regions with elastic labor supplies. The recent shift rates in South Atlantic employment, which we present in Chapter 4, suggest that this is happening already.

Growth in the Pacific region is also reaching limits but of a different sort. Although the demand for labor will probably outstrip the supply in the South Atlantic region, the reverse will probably occur in the Pacific region. If wages were low there, the cycle we outlined above—industry moves in, per-capita incomes rise, workers move in, wages stay low—would result. However, wages are high in the Pacific region, and they have been high for some time. Thus there is no special incentive for disproportionate numbers of jobs to follow migrants to the Pacific region. This makes it difficult for personal income, which in the Pacific region depends heavily on earnings, to increase faster than population, and the resulting decline in per-capita incomes—the beginnings of which we show in Chapter 4—should attenuate endogenous migration somewhat. Coupled with several limits peculiar to parts of the Pacific region—extraordinary housing prices, limits on development, water shortages, and so on—these trends suggest to us, although somewhat less than unequivocally, that growth will slow.

The decelerating regions thus share not a set of detailed trends but, rather, a general limiting of the forces that drove their earlier growth. Although the analyses differ for the two regions, our conclusions are the same: Their growth will slow.

Resurgent Regions

Here again we group two regions because we predict similar futures for them, not because their detailed structure is similar. New England is the archetypal industrial region, West North Central the archetypal agricultural region.

The West North Central region comprises the large farm states of the Midwest, and like most farm areas it has a well-developed system of small towns, counties, and commercial cities. As population shifted toward metropolitan areas, it particularly left the West North Central region for other, more urbanized regions. As we saw above and as Chapter 3 shows, the reversal of the metropolitan flow promises to reverse the migration pattern of this region, if only modestly. Wages in the West North Central region are lower than the national average; only the three southern regions are lower. The raw materials for heavy industry—coal and steel, for example—are close at hand, as are convenient railroad, lake, and river transportation. These factors should combine in a cycle much like the southern one, in which a region attracts both people and jobs without wage increases.

The New England region has low wages as well, but its historically high labor-force participation rates prevent its entering the southern cycle. Unlike most other regions, the structure of New England's economy has changed dramatically, with farming giving way to textiles, textiles giving way to general manufacturing, and this giving way to high technology. New England also has a relatively well-educated labor force, in part because it attracts migrants from other regions not to jobs but to schools. The result of all this is that, with a few exceptions, New England has never grown strongly or suffered heavily. In recent years the nonmetropolitan states of northern New England have attracted population while the technologically advanced industries in southern New England have prospered. These trends should continue, and thus we believe that the modest growth New England's economy experienced during the late 1970s (which we discuss briefly in Chapter 4) will continue into the 1980s. Although the southern New England states may lose some population, the other states will gain enough to offset this through the 1980s. Beyond 1990 the outlook for New England is less optimistic, since the relatively low fertility of young New Englanders will combine with the longevity of elderly ones to produce a rather old population.

This discussion summarizes the implications of our projections for the individual regions. In the next two chapters we explore the regions' economic and demographic histories in some more detail, after which we explore the social and policy implications of our predictions in Chapter 5.

Chapter 3

DEMOGRAPHIC CHANGE:
A CLOSER LOOK

As we discuss regional diversity in demographic growth and look ahead toward even more diversity in the 1980s, it is necessary to keep two points in mind. First, regions are not homogeneous entities, and often the variation within a region is as important as the diversity among regions that we have been emphasizing in this report. Second, we have been able to incorporate only partial data from the 1980 Census.

The extent of variation within regions is evident in the state data for 1950 to 1980 reported in Table 3.1. The contrast between Map 3.1, which illustrates regional population, and Map 3.2, which illustrates state population, emphasizes the point even more clearly for 1980 population. In Table 3.1 New England, where this book is written, provides a good example of the intraregional heterogeneity typical in the nation. The most populous New England state, Massachusetts, has ten times more people than the least populous state, Vermont. In terms of population growth, New England also has a fast-growing subregion analogous to the sectional "sunbelt." This subregion comprises Maine, New Hampshire, and Vermont, where the emigration characteristic of the early decades of this century has slowed and become immigration in the last two decades. Combined with higher-than-average levels of natural increase for the subregion, this shift yields an overall pattern of rapid growth in northern New England. New Hampshire is New England's answer to the West South Central region. Maine's growth pattern mirrors that of the East South Central region: historically slow growth, resulting from high natural increase offset by high net emigration of young adults, followed by

47

Table 3.1 Population by Census Region and State, 1950–1980

Census Region and State	Population (thousands)				Rate of Growth (%)		
	1950	1960	1970	1980	1950–1960	1960–1970	1970–1980
New England	9,315	10,509	11,848	12,349	12.8	12.7	4.2
Maine	914	969	994	1,125	6.0	2.6	13.2
New Hampshire	533	607	738	921	13.9	21.6	24.8
Vermont	378	390	445	511	3.2	14.1	14.8
Massachusetts	4,691	5,149	5,689	5,737	9.8	10.5	0.8
Rhode Island	792	859	950	947	8.5	10.6	−0.3
Connecticut	2,007	2,535	3,032	3,108	26.3	19.6	2.5
East North Central	30,400	36,224	40,262	41,668	19.2	11.1	3.5
Ohio	7,947	9,706	10,657	10,797	22.1	9.8	1.3
Indiana	3,934	4,662	5,195	5,490	18.5	11.4	5.7
Illinois	8,712	10,081	11,110	11,418	15.7	10.2	2.8
Michigan	6,372	7,823	8,882	9,258	22.8	13.5	4.2
Wisconsin	3,435	3,952	4,418	4,705	15.1	11.8	6.5
West North Central	14,062	15,395	16,323	17,183	9.5	6.0	5.3
Minnesota	2,982	3,414	3,806	4,077	14.5	11.5	7.1
Iowa	2,621	2,758	2,825	2,913	5.2	2.4	3.1
Missouri	3,955	4,320	4,678	4,917	9.2	8.3	5.1
North Dakota	620	632	618	653	1.9	−2.2	5.7
South Dakota	653	681	662	690	4.2	−2.8	4.2
Nebraska	1,326	1,411	1,485	1,570	6.4	5.2	5.7
Kansas	1,905	2,179	2,249	2,363	14.4	3.2	5.1

Mid-Atlantic	30,163	34,168	37,209	36,788	13.2	8.9	−1.1
New York	14,830	16,782	18,237	17,557	13.2	8.7	−3.7
New Jersey	4,835	6,067	7,171	7,364	25.5	18.2	2.7
Pennsylvania	10,498	11,319	11,801	11,867	7.8	4.3	0.6
South Atlantic	21,183	25,972	30,678	36,942	22.6	18.1	20.4
Delaware	318	446	548	595	40.3	22.9	8.6
Maryland	2,343	3,101	3,924	4,216	32.4	26.5	7.4
District of Columbia	802	764	757	638	−4.7	−0.9	−15.7
Virginia	3,319	3,967	4,651	5,346	19.5	16.3	14.9
West Virginia	2,006	1,860	1,744	1,950	−7.3	−6.2	11.8
North Carolina	4,062	4,556	5,084	5,874	12.1	11.6	15.5
South Carolina	2,117	2,383	2,591	3,119	12.6	8.7	20.4
Georgia	3,445	3,943	4,588	5,464	14.5	16.4	19.1
Florida	2,771	4,952	6,791	9,740	78.7	37.1	43.4
East South Central	11,478	12,050	12,808	14,663	4.9	6.3	14.5
Kentucky	2,945	3,038	3,221	3,661	3.2	6.0	13.7
Tennessee	3,292	3,567	3,926	4,591	8.4	10.1	16.9
Alabama	3,062	3,267	3,444	3,890	6.7	5.4	13.0
Mississippi	2,179	2,178	2,217	2,521	−0.0	1.8	13.7
West South Central	14,583	16,951	19,326	23,743	16.2	14.0	22.9
Arkansas	1,910	1,786	1,923	2,286	−6.5	7.7	18.9
Louisiana	2,684	3,257	3,645	4,204	21.3	11.9	15.3
Oklahoma	2,233	2,328	2,559	3,025	4.3	9.9	18.2
Texas	7,711	9,580	11,199	14,228	24.2	16.9	27.0

Table 3.1 Population by Census Region and State, 1950–1980 *(continued)*

Census Region and State	Population (thousands)				Rate of Growth (%)		
	1950	1960	1970	1980	1950–1960	1960–1970	1970–1980
Mountain	5,076	6,855	8,289	11,369	35.0	20.9	37.2
Montana	591	675	694	787	14.2	2.8	13.4
Idaho	589	667	713	944	13.7	6.9	32.4
Wyoming	291	330	332	471	13.4	0.6	41.9
Colorado	1,325	1,754	2,210	2,889	32.4	25.9	30.7
New Mexico	681	951	1,017	1,300	39.6	6.9	27.8
Arizona	750	1,302	1,775	2,718	73.6	36.3	53.1
Utah	689	891	1,059	1,461	29.3	18.9	38.0
Nevada	160	285	489	799	78.1	71.6	63.4
Pacific	15,115	21,198	26,553	31,797	40.2	25.3	19.7
Washington	2,379	2,853	3,413	4,130	19.9	19.6	21.0
Oregon	1,521	1,769	2,092	2,633	16.3	18.3	25.9
California	10,586	15,717	19,975	23,669	48.5	27.1	18.5
Alaska	129	226	303	400	75.2	34.1	32.0
Hawaii	500	633	770	965	26.6	21.6	25.3
Total U.S.	151,375	179,322	203,296	226,502	18.5	13.4	11.4

SOURCES: 1970 Census of Population, *General Characteristics*, vol. 1, Table 8; 1980 Census of Population, *Advance Reports*, various state reports.

a dramatic upswing in growth during the 1970s, when the shift from emigration to immigration reinforced growth from natural increase. Vermont is in some ways like the South Atlantic region, where very high natural increase turned suddenly downward during the 1970s. Connecticut's growth pattern mirrors that of the neighboring Mid-Atlantic region, where high natural increase and net immigration combined to bring high growth during the 1950s, but that growth reversed abruptly in the 1970s. By one definition, Vermont is the most rural state in the Union, having not a single city designated as metropolitan. At the other end of this spectrum is Rhode Island, with one of the highest levels of urbanization in the nation. (Rhode Island is demographically unique, having been the only state to lose nonmetropolitan population in the 1970s.) Although New England may be an extreme example of intraregional variability among states, each region is demographically heterogenous on at least several variables.

The second limitation of our analysis to keep firmly in mind is that it has been accomplished with only the most basic of data from the 1980 Census. As we write in June 1981, data which would enable us to determine population accurately by age and sex for states and localities have yet to be released. Such data are necessary to calculate fertility, mortality, and migration rates specific to age and sex groups; these, in turn, are necessary if population projections are to be sensitive to recently observed trends in demographic variables. For this reason, we have not attempted detailed population projections for each region in a formal sense. We focus our efforts instead on understanding *trends* rather than precise *levels*. The reader who needs more detailed population projections must await further analyses of detailed 1980 Census data.

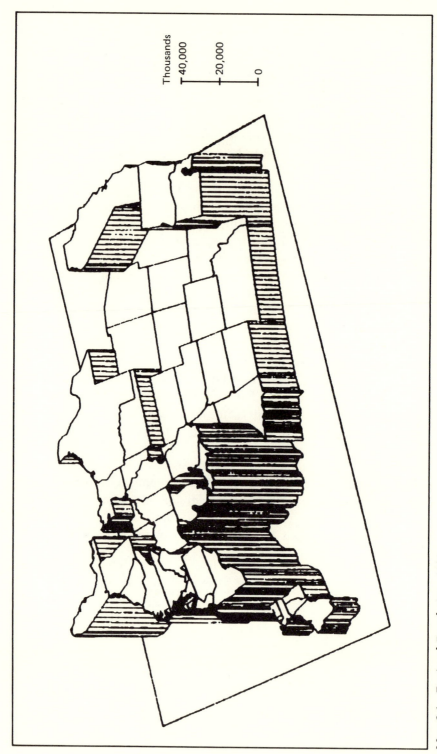

Thousands

40,000

20,000

0

Map 3.1 Regional Population, 1980.

52

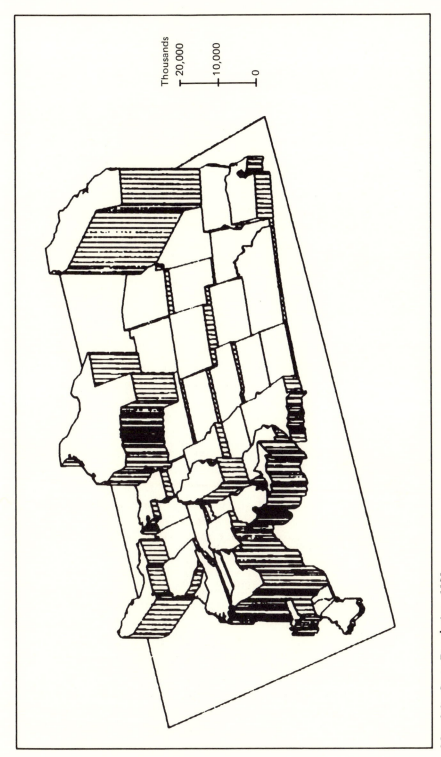

Map 3.2 State Population, 1980.

Thousands

20,000

10,000

0

Diversity in Growth Rates

At the very base of our geographic heterogeneity are the populations of different states and regions and the changes in these numbers that have been taking place in recent years. These changes reflect historical and current differences in the attractiveness of different parts of the country for living, working, and raising families. The aggregate totals by state and region, which appear along with historical data in Table 3.1, are extremely interesting indicators of underlying trends and differences in regional demographic, social, and economic conditions. The four northern regions (New England, East North Central, West North Central, and Mid-Atlantic) grew more slowly than other regions during the 1970s. During this period 18 of the 21 northern states grew less than 10 percent over the decade, with only Maine, New Hampshire, and Vermont exceeding this rate. In contrast, only 2 of the 29 southern and western states (and the District of Columbia) had growth rates under 10 percent between 1970 and 1980. Twenty-seven states grew at rates exceeding 10 percent, including all of the Mountain, Pacific, West South Central, East South Central, and South Atlantic states except Delaware and Maryland.

Among the slow-growing regions, the Mid-Atlantic actually lost population because of New York's negative growth coupled with sharply falling rates of increase in Pennsylvania and New Jersey. The only other state to lose population over the decade was Rhode Island, although Massachusetts and Pennsylvania came close to experiencing negative growth, and Ohio, Illinois, Connecticut, and New Jersey were not far behind. If present trends continue, these six states could very well turn up in the red over the next decade, and they may very well be joined by others, including Indiana, Michigan, Delaware, and Maryland.

The South Atlantic, East South Central, and West South Central regions were big population winners in the 1970s. Between 1970 and 1980 the South increased its share of total United States population from 31 to 33 percent, a gain of 12.5 million people yielding and a growth rate of 20 percent. The jump in the West South Central region's growth rate, led by Texas, is particularly noteworthy, and the high growth in the South Atlantic region, paced by Florida, continues a pattern evident since 1950. Over the past decade the South Atlantic surpassed the Mid-Atlantic as the second most populous region. If present trends continue, the South Atlantic region could supplant the East North Central region as most populous region before the end of this century. Growth was spread unevenly across the South Atlantic region, with Maryland and Florida establishing the lower and upper bounds of 10-year growth at 7 percent and 43 percent, respectively (except for the District of Columbia's 16 percent loss).

The contrasts among growth patterns in the remaining three census regions are the most varied and interesting of all. The West North Central region, over the past 30 years, has demonstrated the greatest homogeneity and stability in growth, with a slow but steady increase of just over 3 million people between 1950 and 1980. The growth rate for this region over the 1970s was about 5 percent, about what it was over the 1960s. The neighboring Mountain region, in contrast, showed the most spectacular growth rates of all. Nevada led all states in the 1970s with a 10-year increase of 64 percent, closely followed by Arizona with 53 percent and Wyoming with 42 percent. At such rates these states' populations would double every 15 to 19 years. The Mountain region has always been the least populous in the nation, but at present growth rates, this region will surpass New England in population well before 1990.

The Pacific region traditionally has had its growth determined by the trend in California, the most populous state in the nation. During the 1950s the Pacific region, paced by California's 40 percent growth, grew more rapidly than any other region. During the 1960s the region held its lead, but its growth rate fell to 25 percent. During the 1970s, the continued decline in California's growth to 18.5 percent caused average growth in the region over the decade to fall to 20 percent (although all other states in the region grew faster than this). During the 1970s, the Pacific region's growth rate fell to fourth, behind the Mountain, West South Central, and South Atlantic regions.

As we shall see below, the underlying mechanisms behind these regional differences in growth patterns are likely to continue present growth trends for a number of years. What is more, variation in growth patterns among individual states is likely to increase to an even greater degree over the next decade, as more states in the North and East follow quickly behind New York and Rhode Island and enter the loss column, and more states in the South

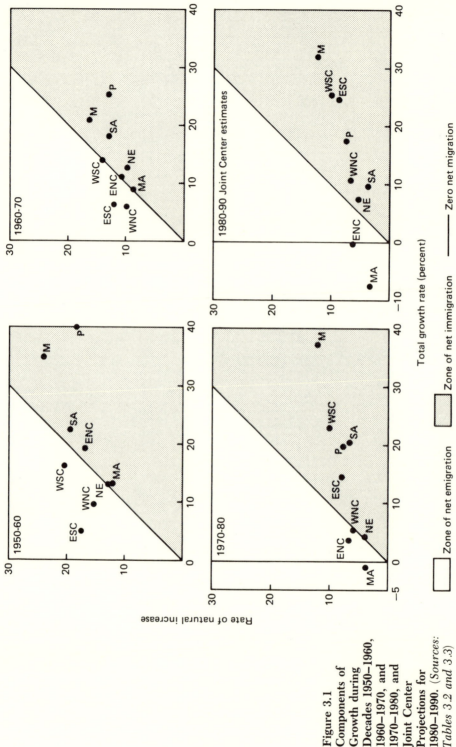

Figure 3.1
Components of
Growth during
Decades 1950–1960,
1960–1970, and
1970–1980, and
Joint Center
Projections for
1980–1990. (*Sources:
Tables 3.2 and 3.3*)

and West follow the Mountain states into sustained spurts of growth. We first discuss the overall balance among components of population growth and then turn to several specific trends: nonmetropolitan growth, cohort and life cycle migration, fertility, age structure, household structure, and ethnic mix.

Components of Population Growth

The number of people living in a region with fixed boundaries can change as a result of two factors: natural increase and net migration. During the 1950s, when fertility rates in all regions of the country were soaring upward, natural increase (births minus deaths) accounted for all or most of the growth in every region except Pacific and Mountain, the only regions where net migration ranked with natural increase in determining levels of growth. The legacy of the post–World War II boom of births is a relatively young population, ensuring that there will continue to be an excess of births over deaths in most regions for the remainder of the century. However, throughout the 1960s and into the 1970s, declining fertility rates have meant declining rates of natural increase, with net migration emerging in the 1970s as an ever more important factor determining whether a region grows rapidly, slowly, or not at all.

Long-Term Trends

The components of population growth in each region over the three decades since 1950 are summarized in Figure 3.1. Each panel of this figure plots total growth against natural increase for the four decades between 1950 and 1990. The line on the diagonal marks the points at which all of the total growth in a region is due solely to an excess of births over deaths—that is, net migration is zero. The area below the diagonal is the zone of net immigration, where the rate of natural increase is less than the rate of total growth. In the area above the diagonal, natural increase is less than total growth, and net migration is therefore negative over the decade.

In the 1950s the post–World War II baby boom pushed regional natural increase up to between 12 and 24 percent, accounting for most growth in all regions of the country except the Pacific. The

East South Central, West South Central, and West North Central regions had negative net migration, with practically all of their losses being picked up by the Mountain and Pacific regions through a series of complex population flows primarily from South to North and from North to West. The New England, East North Central, Mid-Atlantic, and South Atlantic regions picked up net migrants at very modest rates over the decade. Only the Pacific region gained immigrants at a rate sufficient to have the migration rate surpass the rate of natural increase.

Although overall *levels* of growth have been more strongly influenced by natural increase, *variation* in rates due to natural increase has been small, compared with variation in regional migration rates. The reason is that the baby boom and subsequent baby bust extended across all regions, but migration patterns, almost by definition, have varied across regions. The largest difference in rates of natural increase in any of the three decades was between the Mid-Atlantic and Mountain states during the 1950s, a spread from highest to lowest of 11.9 percentage points. By contrast, that same decade saw a spread of 34.4 percentage points in the migration rates (between the East South Central and Pacific regions). During the 1960s, regional variation in natural increase shrank to a maximum difference of only 7.7 percentage points. In the 1970s the spread in natural increase rates was only 8.3 percentage points, compared with a 30 percentage-point spread in the net migration.

Over the 1960s fertility rates and consequently the rates of natural increase declined sharply in all regions. In most regions net migration declined even more sharply. This trend is reflected in Figure 3.1 by the fact that the data points are pulled toward the origin in the 1960–1970 panel. This trend owes its existence to the shift in age and family structure caused by the twentieth-century fertility swing (which we describe below). Natural increase declined between 1960 and 1970. Many couples had already completed their fertility with closely spaced early births during the previous decade. In addition, there were fewer young adults aged 20 to 40, these cohorts having been born during the low-fertility 1920s and 1930s. Migration slowed down because the baby boom of the 1950s had expanded the population in those categories that are the least mobile over long distances: young children and the parents of young children.

The 1970s saw net migration regain its importance in differential growth patterns, a trend apparent in the 1970–1980 panel of Figure 3.1. Natural increase continued to decline across all regions, and the baby-boom generation aged into the life stage where migration rates increase, namely, single adulthood. Over the 1980s the number of single men and women in their late twenties should continue to grow, keeping migration rates high (unless the baby-boom generation suddenly marries and has children—a change that would diminish the influence of net migration in a manner very similar to the trends of the 1960s). Empty-nesters in middle and old age, on the other hand, are expected to increase their numbers in all future demographic scenarios and, depending on their levels of mobility, could set the tone for migration patterns during the remainder of this century and beyond. In the past this group has been relatively immobile. Since empty-nesters are now concentrated in larger suburban homes, however, and tax benefits favor house sales after age 55, the temptation to cash in on unused excess space by moving might prompt new mobility patterns in the future.

The 1950s witnessed substantial emigration from the predominantly rural and less populous East South Central, West South Central, and West North Central regions. The 1960s continued this pattern of rural-urban migration but at lower levels. The South Atlantic and New England regions garnered more immigrants than in the previous decade, while immigration to the East North Central region ground to a complete halt.

The 1970s saw a fundamental change in the migration pattern of the previous decades. The regions that lost emigrants between 1970 and 1980 were the very regions that had attracted immigrants in the immediate post–World War II period, namely, the industrial East North Central and Middle Atlantic regions. Furthermore, the regions that had sent migrants north and east during the era of rapid metropolitan population growth, particularly the East South Central and West South Central regions, gained immigration in the past decade. Even the West North Central farm belt, which lost migrants heavily in the 1950s, almost stemmed the tide of emigration in the 1970s. If recent trends continue, the West North Central region should even gain migrants in the 1980s.

The other three regions (South Atlantic, Pacific, and Mountain) that gained migrants in the 1970s held this position for all three decades covered in Table 3.2, although their pattern of gain was not similar. The South Atlantic region gained migrants moderately

Table 3.2 Components of Rate of Growth by Region, 1950–1980

Region	1950–1960			1960–1970			1970–1980		
	Total Growth	Natural Increase	Net Migration[a]	Total Growth	Natural Increase	Net Migration	Total Growth	Natural Increase	Net Migration
New England	12.8%	12.6%	0.2%	12.7%	9.7%	3.0%	4.2%	4.0%	0.2%
East North Central	19.2	16.9	2.3	11.1	11.5	-0.4	3.5	6.7	-3.2
West North Central	9.5	15.3	-5.8	6.0	9.9	-3.9	5.3	6.0	-.7
Mid-Atlantic	13.2	12.2	1.0	8.9	8.7	0.2	-1.1	3.8	-4.9
South Atlantic	22.6	19.5	3.1	18.1	13.0	5.1	20.4	6.7	13.7
East South Central	4.9	17.5	-12.6	6.3	12.1	-5.8	14.5	8.0	6.5
West South Central	16.2	20.5	-4.3	14.0	14.2	-0.2	22.9	10.1	12.8
Mountain	35.0	24.1	10.9	20.9	16.4	4.5	37.2	12.1	25.1
Pacific	40.2	18.4	21.8	25.3	13.1	12.1	19.7	7.8	11.9

SOURCES: *Statistical Abstract of the United States 1961* and *1972*, Table 8; *Monthly Vital Statistics Report*, various issues 1972 to 1980; *Current Population Reports*, Series P-25, No. 796, Table 4; *Advance Reports*, 1980 Census of Population and Housing.

[a] The net-migration figures are derived as a residual, once total growth and natural increase are established. Since the total growth figures may also include an error term due to differential undercount at either beginning or ending time point (or both), the "net-migration" estimates also include differential undercount. Natural increase is estimated from vital statistics and is generally quite accurate.

in the first two decades, with most states' losses of young job seekers to northern states more than offset by retirement migration of older people to one state, Florida. In the last decade not only did the exodus of young people slow and even reverse, but other southern states besides Florida became attractive places for people to spend the final years of their lives.

The aging of the United States population over the next 50 years could be a potent force in the future for those states and regions for which retirement migration is significant. However, as long as the trend is toward greater diversity in choices of location for retirement, as it appears to be, none will ever grow as much as Florida did in previous decades. The impact on Florida was cumulative. This state, for more than two decades, was almost the sole recipient of moderate retiree flows from many northern states. The emigration rates of old people from sending states are not expected to change dramatically in the decades to come. If the movers distribute themselves more evenly around the country, the gains in individual receiving states will be modest. The real future of growth due to migration, as is usual, lies with the behavior of young people, for whom migration rates are high. If the southern states can attract young immigrants and hold on to the native young, the recent spurt in the growth there can be sustained for the remainder of this century. However, as we suggested in earlier chapters, this may be impossible in some regions.

The migration flow to the Pacific region, also a region with net immigration over all three decades, was almost the mirror image of the pattern in the South Atlantic region. The most rapid regional growth ever recorded occurred in the Pacific region during the 1950s: almost 22 percent growth due to migration and over 18 percent due to natural increase. The next decade saw a sharp drop in the Pacific net migration rate, with the rate during the last decade remaining approximately stable at a substantial 12 percent.

The Mountain states exhibited the most volatile immigration pattern over the three-decade period. High immigration during the 1950s was followed by a sharp plunge in the migration rate, which was in turn followed by the sharpest rise in growth due to migration of any region, from 4.5 percent in the 1960s to 25.1 percent in the 1970s. Why migration to the Mountain region dropped so sharply in the 1960s is not clear.

Table 3.3 Projected Components of Growth by Region, 1980–1990: Census Bureau II-B Projections and Joint Center Projections (numbers in thousands)

| | Census II-B Projections 1980–1990[a] | | | | | | Joint Center Projections 1980–1990 | | | | | |
| | Total Growth | | Natural Increase | | Net Migration | | Total Growth | | Natural Increase | | Net Migration | |
Region	Percent	Number	Percent	Number	Percent	Number	Percent	Number	Percent	Number	Percent	Number
New England	8.3	1039	6.8	849	1.5	190	7.3	901	5.5	679	1.8	222
East North Central	4.5	1868	8.5	3510	-4.0	1642	-0.4	-166	6.3	2625	-6.7	-2791
West North Central	6.3	1077	7.4	1259	-1.1	-182	10.6	1821	6.7	1151	3.9	670
Mid-Atlantic	2.5	918	5.5	2047	-3.0	-1129	-7.6	-2795	3.5	1288	-11.1	-4083
South Atlantic	16.9	6188	7.2	2641	9.7	3547	9.6	3547	3.8	1404	5.8	2143
East South Central	10.0	1416	7.7	1092	2.4	324	24.5	3593	8.7	1276	15.8	23.7
West South Central	13.7	3051	9.9	2192	3.8	859	25.3	6007	10.0	2374	15.3	3633
Mountain	20.7	2220	12.0	1281	8.7	939	31.9	3627	12.5	1421	19.4	2206
Pacific	12.0	3572	8.5	2531	3.5	1041	16.4	5215	7.6	2417	8.8	2798
Total U.S.	9.6	21,353	7.9	17,405	1.8	3,948	9.6	21,750	6.5	14,635	3.1	7,115

[a] Growth rates calculated on projected 1980 base for Census II-B and actual 1980 Census count for Joint Center estimates.

1980s Trends

The differences between the projected components of growth for the 1980s according to Census II-B projections and Joint Center projections are given in Table 3.3. Although total growth over the decade in both series is projected to be about 9.6 percent, the proportion due to natural increase is higher in the Census series than it is in the Joint Center projections. Much larger differences appear in the projected growth pattern of the individual regions. The largest differences are in the West South Central and Mid-Atlantic regions. In the former, the Census projects almost 3 million fewer residents in 1990 than we do, the difference being almost entirely due to lower net migration in the Census II-B series. The difference in projected growth in the Mid-Atlantic is in the opposite direction, with natural increase as well as net migration being substantially higher in the Census series.

Another region showing a large difference in the projected growth pattern is East South Central, where projected net migration into the area over the 1980s is almost 2 million lower in the Census series. The higher level of net migration we foresee for the next decade is the result of increased retirement migration into the area. Some people left the East South Central region as young workers during the 1950s and will return to their "roots." The general attractiveness of the nonmetropolitan areas in this region will draw other immigrants. This same pattern of growth is expected in the West North Central states over the next decade but to a lesser degree because of the less favorable climate.

We forecast that the population of the East North Central region will decline slightly, compared with the 4.5 percent growth in the Census series projects. This difference arises because we expect a lower rate of natural increase and a higher rate of net emigration than Census projections do. In fact, the two components of growth are likely to be of roughly equal magnitude but opposite sign. High emigration could place Ohio, Illinois, and Michigan in the loss column for total population over the next decade. Growth in Indiana and Wisconsin should be modest but insufficient to balance losses elsewhere in the region.

Finally, growth in the Mountain and Pacific regions is projected to be in the same direction according to both our projections and the Census series, but we expect natural increase and net migration to be higher than the Census does. Even though the future trajectories of these two regions are relatively uncertain because of past fluctuations in growth rates, the Census series appears to be too low by at least 5 percent.

The Revival of Nonmetropolitan Growth

A distinctive aspect of population growth in the 1970s has been the resurgence of nonmetropolitan areas. This trend was first recognized in the early 1970s, and considerable effort has been devoted over the past five years to measuring its magnitude and explaining its origins.[1] This work has been summarized nicely by Long and DeAre,[2] and new data from the 1980 Census have been incorporated into a recent analysis by Beale.[3]

For most of the twentieth century, population movements served to concentrate people in what demographers now call "Standard Metropolitan Statistical Areas" (SMSAs). SMSAs are groupings of contiguous counties around a core county containing a central city of at least 50,000 population. Contiguous counties are included if there is significant integration with the core county, as measured by commuting of its population into the core area for employment. Of the 3,143 counties in the United States, 678, or 21.5 percent, were classified as metropolitan in 1980. This number is likely to increase by about 50 counties on the basis of the employment data in the 1980 Census. Although under 25 percent of all counties in the United States are metropolitan, a majority of the population lives in SMSAs. In 1980 approximately 166 million of a total of 226.5 million people, or 73 percent, lived in metropolitan counties. In 1970, 74.2 percent of the population lived in the same counties (although some of them were not yet classified as metropolitan counties).

The proportion of the population classified as metropolitan can change as a result of three processes: (1) natural increase in and net migration to places already designated as metropolitan; (2) the annexation of adjacent nonmetropolitan counties to metropolitan areas because of the integration of the labor force into the metropolitan employment sector; and (3) the reclassification of whole nonmetropolitan areas as metropolitan because a central city's population exceeds 50,000 residents.

Through 1970, metropolitan counties grew more rapidly than

nonmetropolitan ones. Figure 3.2 shows this to be so in seven of the nine regions. For most of this period the first process cited above was the major engine driving metropolitan growth. During the 1960s, when birth rates in metropolitan areas were still high and people were still migrating in great numbers from farms and small towns to cities, metropolitan areas grew by 17 percent and nonmetropolitan areas by only 4.4 percent. During the 1970s, by contrast, metropolitan grew by 9.1 percent while the population classified as nonmetropolitan grew by 15.4 percent. What is more significant, recent metropolitan growth is almost entirely due to annexation and reclassification of nonmetropolitan counties. Low levels of natural increase and substantial emigration from existing metropolitan areas caused these places to lose population on average. Only among southern and certain Mountain states did metropolitan areas experience major gains in population.

The other important story told by Figure 3.2, in addition to the sustained decline in metropolitan growth in most regions between 1950 and 1980, is the resurgence in nonmetropolitan growth, indicated by the upswing in the dotted line in the 1970–1980 decade. Only in New England did nonmetropolitan growth take a slight turn downward, but this was almost entirely due to nonmetropolitan loss in Rhode Island, which in turn reflected the closing of a major naval base. (Small events have large effects in small places.) In addition, the slowdown in nonmetropolitan growth in Connecticut more than offset increases in nonmetropolitan population in the other four New England states.[4]

It is now clear that revived nonmetropolitan growth is a new force shaping the structure of the United States population, but the underlying causes of this growth are less clear. Part is simply spillover of metropolitan population into adjacent nonmetropolitan areas that have not yet changed definition. These are often places to which jobs as well as people are moving, but growth in others is exclusively residential.

The more remote of the nonadjacent nonmetropolitan areas are now attracting migrants, after decades of net emigration. When asked, most of these migrants give employment-related reasons for the move. Yet many of the remote nonmetropolitan destinations appear to offer less in the way of economic opportunities than the areas migrants leave behind. This has led many analysts to conclude that, whatever the espoused reasons for moving, factors other than employment opportunities, such as leisure or re-

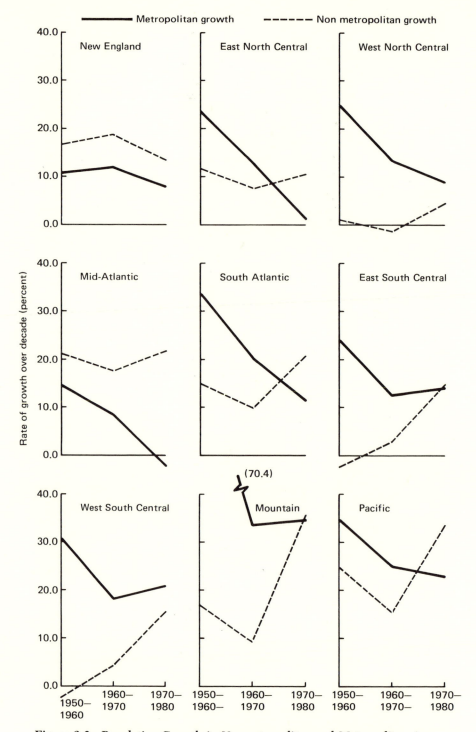

Figure 3.2 Population Growth in Nonmetropolitan and Metropolitan Areas during Decades 1950–1960, 1960–1970, and 1970–1980.

tirement lifestyles, are important for the new migration patterns. Many nonmetropolitan counties offer unusually attractive economic opportunities, particularly if they are near new energy projects, and others appear to offer a balance among economic, family, and leisure opportunities. Still others are attractive simply because of their remoteness; many people frustrated with urban life will endure significant economic, cultural, and social deprivation for short periods in order to get away.

Survey data can go only so far in helping us to understand the revival of nonmetropolitan growth. Normally a positive turnaround in net migration, such as the one we have observed for nonmetropolitan areas during this past decade, begins with a decline in emigration and only later includes significant immigration to the area. Therefore, in order fully to understand the shift, it is necessary to understand why individuals who might have moved away in the past have decided to stay put. Those individuals and their motivations for not migrating are usually not the subjects of migration studies. Unemployment and housing prices simply may have made the perceived chances of finding a good job and inexpensive housing in the city too slim. Genuine new employment opportunities have been emerging at the same time in nonmetropolitan areas, and the hometown folks are the first to know about and act on them. As these opportunities expand and as word of them gets around, new immigrants will arrive on the scene, and the nonmetropolitan revival will enter its later phase.

Net Migration: Cohort and Life Cycle

Net migration trends have differed markedly over the past three decades. The composition and significance of these patterns can best be understood in terms of the interregional shifts of population of different ages, or life cycle stages. The fact that patterns of migration have varied significantly across age groups has altered substantially the overall regional location of different "birth cohorts," or populations born in different years. The cohort migration patterns reveal sharp but not surprising variations in net migration flows observed at different stages in the life cycle.

All of our analysis in this section is based on *net* changes in the location of cohorts between time periods. Thus, for example, we compare the location of the 25- to 29-year-olds in 1970 with that of the 15- to 19-year-olds in 1960. Measured in this way, shifts in geographic distribution may reflect not only interregional migration but also interregional differences in international migration and in mortality. Interregional migration flows are the dominant influence. We say nothing directly about the size or direction of the gross migration flows. The shift of a particular cohort out of a particular region, for example, could result either from a large outflow and a smaller but still large inflow or from a small outflow counterbalanced by a negligible inflow. A region that holds a constant share of a particular cohort over time may in fact be a way station between regions losing and gaining populations. Instead of looking at these gross migration flows, we will focus intentionally on the net effects of population redistribution on particular regions and cohorts.

The net effects of interregional migration flows can be seen in Figure 3.3. The figure is complex, since it contains information on ten age groups in nine regions over three decades, and it is helpful to discuss it briefly before we turn to its content. Each regional panel contains a series of lines whose level gives the proportion of a cohort living in the region for up to 30 years (1950 to 1980). In Mid-Atlantic, for example, we have flagged the cohort born 1921–1925. Approximately 20 percent of these people lived in the Mid-Atlantic region in 1950 (when they were 25 to 29 years old), in 1960 (when they were 35 to 39) and in 1970 (when they were 45 to 49). This constancy indicates that for every member of that cohort who moved out of the Mid-Atlantic region over those two decades, another member of the same cohort must have moved in. Between 1970 and 1980 the proportion of this cohort living in the Mid-Atlantic region declined, indicating that more moved out than moved in. If there had been no net movement in or out of a region over the entire 1950–1980 period, the cohort trends would be perfectly horizontal. The New England region comes closest to this scenario.

It was not only individuals in the 1921–1925 cohort who moved away from the Mid-Atlantic states during the 1970s, as the downturns in the right ends of all the cohort trajectories in this panel show. The 1970s brought multi-cohort net emigration to the East North Central region as well. The upward sloping trajectories in the Pacific region show that, unlike the Mid-Atlantic and East North Central regions, the Pacific region gained migrants, especially during the 1950s, with some leveling off in the 1970s indicated by the flatter rightmost segment of the cohort lines. The West South Central region shows the turnaround from falling cohort trajectories during the 1950s to rising cohort trajectories during the 1970s. The same turnaround in migration occurred in the East South Central region, but it is harder to see in Figure 3.3 because the upward sloping 1970–1980 trends are buried in the 1950–1970 data points. The Mountain states show a rise in cohort trends throughout the 30-year period, with the sharpest increase coming in the last decade.

The most complex trends in cohort migration are those represented in the South Atlantic region. During the 1950s, emigration of young cohorts was counterbalanced by immigration of older cohorts. During the 1960s, the emigration of younger cohorts began to turn around, and by the 1970s all cohorts showed upward-sloping trajectories.

It is clear from the South Atlantic's experience that the aggregate rate of net migration, which lumps age groups together, conceals major variations in the migration of the population at different stages of the life cycle. The underlying complex of offsetting trends represented in this panel reveals much about the nature of past population movements. This is helpful in making forecasts but, given the erratic patterns of net cohort regional migration and other information about regional shifts, is hardly the sole basis for firm projections.

Certain broad migration patterns are likely to continue, of course. Differences of climate and cost of living make it highly likely that the persistent movements of retirement-age population from the East North Central and Mid-Atlantic regions into the South Atlantic, West South Central, Mountain, and Pacific regions will continue at some level. Also, the huge development potential of the West argues for continued inflows of young adults to this region, although distributions within the West are hard to predict.

Beyond these patterns, however, there is little basis for knowing whether past trends will persevere, accelerate, or attenuate. Migration, for example, continued to be erratic in the 1970s. The first counts of the 1980 Census indicate that the earlier tendencies of young adults to leave the South Central regions for the East North Central region were totally reversed during the 1970s. The net flows south are so substantial that they must comprise young and retired adults going in the same direction, instead of offsetting each other as they did in the past.

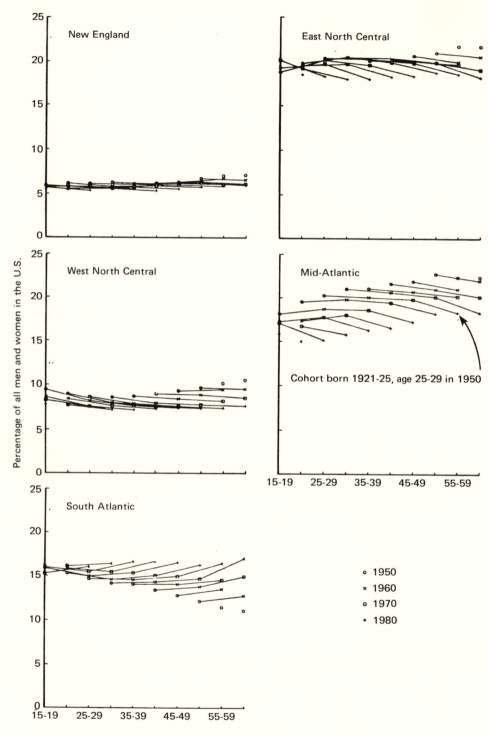

Cohort born 1921-25, age 25-29 in 1950

Percentage of all men and women in the U.S.

Age in years

New England

East North Central

West North Central

Mid-Atlantic

South Atlantic

○ 1950
× 1960
□ 1970
♦ 1980

70

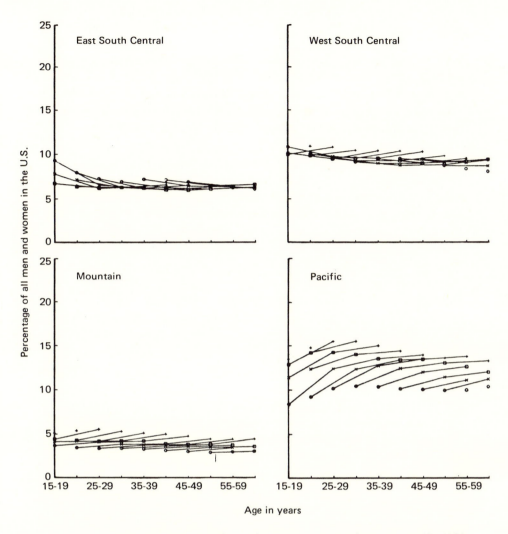

Figure 3.3   Interregional Migration Flows of Cohorts, Men and Women, 1950–1980.

Thus the volatility of regional net migration patterns between 1950 and 1970 did not abate during the past decade, and it complicates the task of projecting future migration flows. Our schematic model in Chapter 2 and the historical analysis in Chapter 4 give us some insight into the causes of these fluctuations. The reversals of the migration flows in the West South Central and East North Central regions seem to be associated with the growth of petroleum and other extractive industries in the former region and the decline of heavy industry in the latter, whereas the new patterns in the Mid-Atlantic, East South Central, and West North

71

Central regions are apparently linked with economic decline, the emergence of a strong rural drift of population in the 1970s, and the basic labor requirements of agricultural industries. The future course of population movements will depend both on the continued strength of these forces and on the emergence of major new forces during the 1980s.

Net population movements between 1950 and 1980 generally reduced interregional differences in age distributions. Regions with proportionally large numbers of teenagers in 1950 and 1960— the agricultural West North Central, East South Central, and West South Central states—lost young adults. Similarly, regions with concentrations of older adults—New England, the Mid-Atlantic, and the two North Central regions—experienced large outflows of older adults. The South Atlantic regions, which had a relatively small older population in 1950, had substantial increases in this part of their age distribution. At the same time, the convergence of fertility rates in different regions, described in the next section, further narrowed regional variations in the age distribution by eliminating the legacy of earlier high fertility, or concentrations of teenagers in the West North Central, South Atlantic, and two South Central regions.

The historical convergence of regional age distributions resulted from a confluence of circumstances unlikely to be repeated in the coming decade. Foremost among these circumstances was the enormous, unprecedented shift of retirement-age population to the South Atlantic regions, which, because of past migration and fertility patterns, had a substantial relative scarcity of older adults in 1950. There does not appear to have been any causal relationship between the initial regional age imbalances per se and subsequent patterns of migration; instead, portable Social Security income (and other pensions), cheap air conditioning, easy air travel, attractive house-price differentials, and lower costs of living drew older immigrants south. Another major contribution to the convergence of regional age distributions, the departure of young adults from the southern regions with a relative surplus of teenagers, declined as the regional concentration of teenagers did. The surplus of teenagers may have impeded their entry into the local labor market, thereby predisposing them to migrate once they were able to do so.

Although future disparities in the regional distribution of young adults could one day produce another convergent migration pattern, none is projected to arise until after 1990. Rather, current trends in age-specific relocation are more likely to make regional age distributions *diverge* from one another in the future. In particular, if retiree migration to the South Atlantic region continues to exceed young-adult immigration there, a regional concentration of retirement-age people will result. Symmetrically, if westward immigrants continue to be disproportionately young, the age distribution in the Mountain and Pacific regions will skew toward young adults and those in mid–working life, and continued high fertility among these groups will increase the size of later young cohorts. There does not, in general, seem to be an equilibrating mechanism that brings regional age distributions toward the norm.

Fertility

The fertility swing following World War II was marked by a convergence of fertility rates across regions through the boom side of the cycle and into the beginning of the downswing, followed by a divergence among regional rates on the bust side. As Figure 3.4 shows, in 1940 the *total fertility rate* (TFR), a measure of current fertility, was about 1.6 births per woman. It then rose steadily to 3.65 in 1960 before falling in 10 years to 2.48 births per woman, an average decline over the decade of 3.2 percent per year. Between 1970 and 1976 the national birth rate fell at an even more rapid pace, about 5 percent per year, to a low of 1.74, substantially below the 2.1 births per woman needed for replacement. Since 1976 the TFR has fluctuated slightly, with the general trend upward. Preliminary estimates of the TFR for 1980 place it around 1.87, implying an average annual increase since 1976 of about 1.7 percent.[5] In 1960 the maximum regional TFR difference was between the Mid-Atlantic region (TFR = 3.37) and the Mountain region (TFR = 4.12), with the TFR in all other regions falling between 3.5 and 4.0 births per woman. Between 1960 and 1970 these differentials had narrowed even more: The 1970 Mid-Atlantic TFR was 2.40 and the Mountain TFR was 2.77, a difference of only about a third of a child per woman. State-by-state variation was similarly compressed by 1970, with Connecticut on the low end and Utah on the high end, separated by less than one child per woman.

By 1970 the trend toward divergence was already well estab-

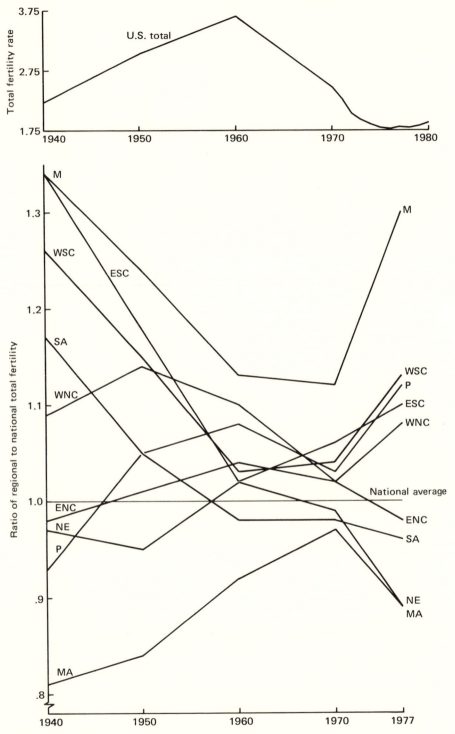

Figure 3.4 Ratios of Regional to National Total Fertility Rates, 1940–1977, and Total Fertility Rate, 1940–1980.

lished, as Figure 3.4 shows, and by 1977 the gap between Connecticut's (the lowest) and Utah's (the highest) total fertility rates was two children per woman. For the most part, fertility patterns (as opposed to levels) have been uniform across regions, with some notable but minor deviations. Since about 1973, the regions in the West have shown an early propensity to level out and increase, while other regions continued their decline until later in the decade. The higher fertility in the West may be due to the influence of Hispanic and Mormon fertility patterns or to earlier or perhaps nontraditional childbearing; this is uncertain for the present. Likewise, the across-the-board increase in fertility by region since 1976 could be interpreted either as the beginning of a new trend or as the result of equilibrating forces balancing the especially sharp declines during the early 1970s. Fertility levels in the late 1970s certainly are more in line with longer-term secular levels of fertility (and with the historical fertility differentials in the 1.7–2.4 range).

The total fertility rate is influenced by two aspects of childbearing: (1) how many children the average woman is having, and (2) when in her reproductive ages she is having those children. Regional differences in fertility have been affected by both these parameters, with timing currently very significant. Because the bulge of the baby-boom generation, born between 1957 and 1962, is now between the ages of 18 and 24, a pattern of early childbearing in a region (say, before age 25) would tend to raise temporarily both the TFR and the total number of births in that region above the trend line, whereas the opposite would be true for a region with a delayed childbearing pattern. In fact, as Figure 3.5 shows, there are significant differences between regions in the timing of fertility. With the exclusion of black women, whose regional differences in the timing pattern of fertility are small in comparison with other women's, the East South Central, West South Central, and South Atlantic regions exhibit higher-than-average fertility during the early part of the reproductive ages and lower-than-average fertility in the later part. The New England and Mid-Atlantic states show the exact opposite pattern, with fertility below the average before age 25 and above average after age 25. The Mountain and Pacific regions have age-specific fertility levels above the national average at all ages. Given these regional differences in the timing of fertility, natural increase will vary according to the childbearing pattern in each region.

Because of the tendency of women living in the East North Central, New England, and Mid-Atlantic regions to postpone

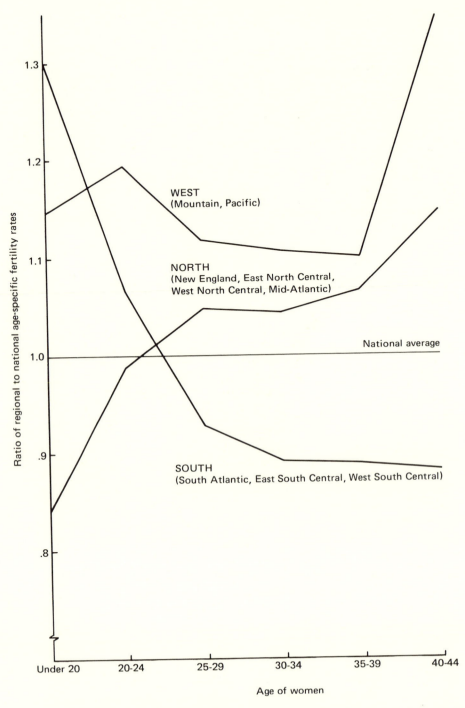

Figure 3.5   Ratios of Regional to National Age-Specific Fertility Rates, 1970–1975
(White and other non-Black races only).

childbearing to their mid-twenties, even during the best of times, the recession of the early 1970s left these regions with an especially strong decline in the level of natural increase. During the 1980s, the bulge of the baby-boom generation passes through the middle and late twenties, the ages when fertility in these late-childbearing regions has traditionally been the greatest. Because women living in the rest of the country have had higher fertility in their early twenties, which the bulge of the baby-boom generation reached during the late 1970s and early 1980s, fertility levels among these women, as they pass through their late twenties during the 1980s in these early-childbearing regions, are expected to fall relative to the gains in the North.

The distinction between "period" and "cohort" fertility is important in deciphering and forecasting trends. Although fertility in the North could equal or even surpass the national average for a brief time during the middle or late 1980s, that does not mean that the actual number of children women have by the end of their reproductive ages will be higher than the national average. In fact, we expect cohort fertility in the North to be substantially below the average for other regions. In the earlier Joint Center Outlook Report *The Nation's Families: 1960–1990,* we estimated that for the nation as a whole, 45 to 50 percent of women born between 1955 and 1960 would end their reproductive ages being childless or having borne only one child.[6] Because of differences in cohort fertility between the North and the rest of the country, the percentages in the New England and Mid-Atlantic regions could be above the 50 percent level, with 20 to 25 percent of this cohort expected to remain childless and another 25 to 30 percent ending their reproductive careers having contributed only one child to the region's natural increase.

Changing Age Structure

Up to this point we have focused on demographic behavior that has changed markedly and differentially in the nine Census regions since 1960. Our glance into the future has been based on how we believe people will adjust their migration and fertility behavior in each region over the next 10 years. Since both migration and fertility have proved to be inherently unstable in the past, the task of predicting these dimensions of demographic behavior in the future is somewhat tenuous.

Another aspect of demographic change, however, is at least as important as growth per se: shifts in the age structure, which result from the simple aging of a population in an area whose age structure has been made uneven by certain historical events. Like immigration and fertility, age structure has changed markedly over the past several decades and will continue to do so over the next, but it is much more predictable. The post–World War II baby boom and baby bust created uneven age structures everywhere in the United States. As the boom cohorts and bust cohorts have succeeded each other in the age structure, this disorderly cohort flow has had important consequences for health care, public schooling, higher education, housing, employment, productivity, recreation, and retirement. Unevenness in the age structure has also had a profound influence on the sociological realities of our times—on such things as the transition to adulthood, sex roles, the nature of work, and the process of family formation and parenthood.

Figure 3.6 compares observed changes in six 10-year age groups of adults for the 1970s with expected change according to Census II-B projections for the 1980–1990 period (the age structure of actual future trends should be much like that of the Census projections). We have excluded the population under 15 years of age in order to avoid the more complex problems with fertility projections; only migration and mortality will affect the trends in those 15 and older over the next 15 years. Although the migration that will take place over the projection period will be different than the Census Bureau assumed, most age-structure change in store for the regions is implicit in their current uneven age structure. We present the Census projections as a first approximation to future age structures and indicate where the projected change seems too high or too low on the basis of our previous analysis of most likely migration trends.

Between 1960 and 1980 the baby-boom generation came of age. The group aged 15 to 24 increased by almost 47 percent over the first decade of this period as the leading edge of the baby boom moved into young adulthood. The 1970s saw a further growth of 20 percent in this age group (indicated by a solid horizontal line in Figure 3.6) as the bulge of the baby boom, born 1957 to 1963, edged its way into this age group. The largest increases in this age group were in the regions that grew through migration over the decade, the lowest in the regions with net emigration.

Over the next 10 years the trend in the 15- to 24-year-olds in the nation as a whole and in each region will be in the opposite direction. Census II-B projections call for a decline of 16.4 percent over the 1980s, although actual trends in foreign immigration will be likely to reduce this figure to 12 percent or so. This switch from growth to decline in the 15–24 age group reflects the decline we described in the preceding section and will be greatest where the fertility declines have been greatest or emigration of fertile young adults has occurred. The largest decline, therefore, will be in the Mid-Atlantic region, where this age group will probably shrink by 25 percent. In contrast, the Mountain region should have about the same number of 15- to 24-year-olds, given its higher fertility in the late 1960s and its growing popularity as a destination for young migrants. In any case, the strong growth in the entry-level labor force to which we have become accustomed over the past two decades will reverse itself in most regions during the 1980s, presenting a strong challenge to employers who have had a ready supply of inexpensive, inexperienced labor.

The 25–34 age group expanded very rapidly during the 1970s—no surprise, since the 15–24 age group had done so a decade earlier. The aging of the leading edge of the baby-boom generation into the next older age group will sharply reduce further increases in the 25–34 age group, from about 50 percent over the 1970s to about 15 percent over the 1980s. Foreign immigration of workers could push the latter figure up to 20 percent or so. With such high growth in the West South Central, Mountain, and Pacific regions during the previous decade, the relative growth during the next decade in these regions must necessarily slow down somewhat but perhaps not as much as indicated in the second panel in Figure 3.6.

The 35–44 age group will experience the greatest amount of relative growth over the next decade. The cohorts in this group in 1970 were those born from 1925 to 1935, a period of very low fertility. Between 1970 and 1980 this age group increasingly consisted of those born between 1935 and 1945, a slightly larger set of cohorts than the former ones. But between 1980 and 1990, the 1935–1945 cohorts will age into the next oldest age group and be replaced by those born from 1945 to 1955, the leading edge of the baby boom. Once again the pattern of growth over the 1980s is likely to be less uniform than implied in the Census II-B projections, with major gains occurring in the South and West.

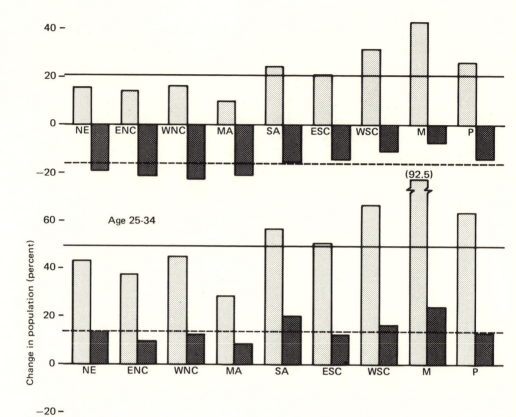

60 –   Age 15-24

40 –

20 –

0

−20 –

(92.5)

60 –   Age 25-34

Change in population (percent)

40 –

20 –

0

NE ENC WNC MA SA ESC WSC M P

−20 –

60 –   Age 35-44

40 –

20 –

0

NE ENC WNC MA SA ESC WSC M P

−20 –

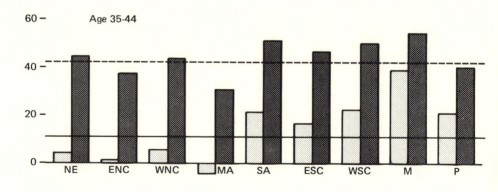

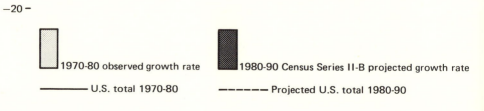

1970-80 observed growth rate   1980-90 Census Series II-B projected growth rate

————— U.S. total 1970-80   ------- Projected U.S. total 1980-90

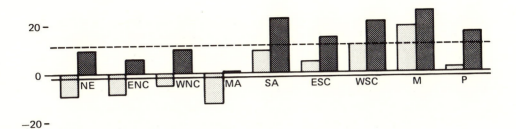

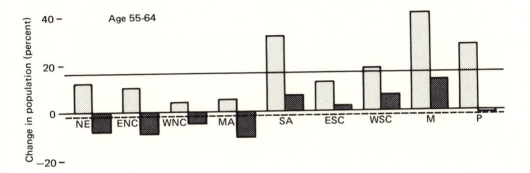

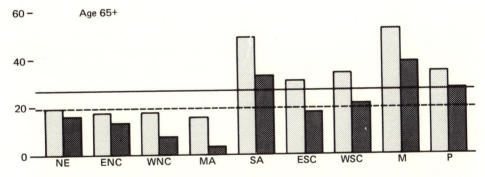

Figure 3.6 Population Growth by Age Group, 1970–1980 and 1980–1990.

This rapid projected increase of the 35–44 age group will pose new problems for the labor force, especially with regard to promotion policies. During the 1980s employers will face simultaneously the need to direct resources toward the recruitment of scarce younger workers and the demands of numerous middle-aged workers for raises and promotions after years of service. All in all, this demographic dynamic in the 15–44 age groups will be like nothing employers have experienced in the recent past.

The three age groups we have considered thus far are expected to grow through the 1980s at rates that are more than 30 percent different from their rates of growth through the 1970s. The next three age groups will break this pattern of extreme change: The cohorts involved all precede the baby boom and are of more similar size. The 45–54 age group declined ever so slightly in size for the United States as a whole during the 1970–1980 period. Variation in growth patterns among regions reflected historical differences in cohort size, as well as the migration patterns of these cohorts when they were 25–34 (during the 1950s) and 35–44 (during the 1960s); we presented but did not discuss these detailed trends in Figure 3.3. The basic regional differentials should hold through the 1980s, with the 45–54 age group as a whole increasing by 11.5 percent, according to Census projections. With the larger-than-expected size of the 35–44 age group in the 1980 Census taken into account, the actual U.S. total increase in 45- to 54-year-olds is going to be closer to 15 percent, and most of these additional persons will appear in the Mountain, South Atlantic, West South Central, and Pacific regions. Instead of the projected 20 to 25 percent increase in these regions, the increase will be 30 percent or slightly more. The Mid-Atlantic and East North Central segments of this age group will grow more slowly than the Census Bureau projects, because of the accelerated movement of the 35–44 age group out of these regions during the late 1970s.

The 55–64 age group is expected to slow its growth nationally through the 1980s decade because of a historical event: the closing of United States borders to the large streams of southern European immigrants during the late 1920s. During the 1980s the 55–64 age group will be composed increasingly of native-born Americans. Since these natives were born during the low-fertility 1920s and early 1930s, their cohort size is relatively small. The Census II-B projections show an actual *decline* in the size of the 55–64 age group over the 1980s. This may be premature, since persons in this age range seem to be improving their longevity more than Census expected them to. A modest increase of 4 or 5 percent in the 55–64 age group is not likely.

The growth trend in the 65+ age group once again shows modest regional differences consistent with the higher overall growth experienced and projected in the South and West. Once again, improvements in life expectancy greater than those incorporated into Census projections will probably result in 1980–1990 trends more closely approximating the 1970–1980 observed trends. In any case, the next decade should not see trends in the 65+ age group very different from the trends of the previous decade. This is therefore the only age where the patterns of change will be consistent over the two decades between 1970 to 1990.

Household and Family Structure

One of the most important demographic changes in the United States since World War II has been in household and living arrangements. An earlier Joint Center Outlook Report, *The Nation's Families: 1960–1990*, described this change in detail for the aggregate United States. The main thrust of this change has been a tremendous growth in households not organized around a married couple. These new households are headed by never-married young adults (some with children); the divorced and separated, with and without young children; and widows, who increasingly head their own households into advanced old age and who usually live alone. For every household headed by an unmarried individual in 1950, almost eight were headed by married couples. By 1980 this ratio was one to two, and by 1990 it is projected almost to even out.

These changes result from two trends that, although they are distinct, reinforce one another. The first is the increasing fraction of the total population that is unmarried, an increase variously attributable to changing age structures; to marriage, divorce, and remarriage rates; and to differential mortality. The second trend underlying the rise of the nonfamily households is the increasing attractiveness of independent living arrangements to the unmarried population. Although much attention has been focused in the media and elsewhere on the first trend, particularly on the consequences of delayed marriage and rising divorce rates, the trends in headship have had a far more substantial effect on overall household structure.

Regional variation in household structure and living arrangements has been difficult to track, particularly during the 1970s, because intercensal sample surveys, such as the Current Population Survey, are too small to permit detailed subnational analysis. However, from the limited information we do have available, it appears that differentials in household and family structure among

Table 3.4   Trends in Headship Rates among Unmarried Women in the New England and Pacific Regions, 1950–1975

	1950	1960	1970	1975
Pacific Region				
15–24	.0467	.0674	.1070	.1283
25–30	.3696	.5450	.6406	.7081
35–44	.5601	.7029	.7523	.8362
45–54	.6164	.7064	.7793	.8169
55–64	.5890	.6762	.7697	.8179
65 +	.5226	.6080	.6614	.7043
New England Region				
15–24	.0123	.0402	.0661	.0994
25–34	.1445	.3070	.4858	.6330
35–44	.3301	.4814	.6140	.7247
45–54	.4852	.5722	.6734	.7256
55–64	.5225	.6094	.7023	.7454
65 +	.4443	.5384	.6011	.6548
Ratio, Pacific/New England				
15–24	3.80	1.68	1.62	1.29
25–34	2.56	1.78	1.32	1.12
35–44	1.70	1.46	1.23	1.15
45–54	1.27	1.23	1.19	1.13
55–64	1.13	1.11	1.10	1.10
65 +	1.18	1.13	1.10	1.08

regions, like fertility, first converged toward a national "average" and then in the late 1970s began to diverge. This pattern is consistent with (and may partly explain) the pattern of divergence among fertility rates. We cannot develop a full description of regional differences in household structure and living arrangements without detailed 1980 Census results. Instead, we will illustrate some likely features of this future analysis by focusing on independent living arrangements among unmarried women in two disparate regions of the country, New England and Pacific, where the trends have been most striking. Table 3.4 presents data on the proportion of all unmarried women of different ages who headed their own households in these two regions for the period between 1950 and 1975.

In 1950 the level of headship among unmarried women in New England under the age of 35 was at most half the levels in the Pacific region. Women over 35 also had substantially lower levels of independent living in New England. Between 1950 and 1975, however, cohorts of unmarried women in New England greatly increased their headship rates, substantially closing the gap between them and their Pacific counterparts. In both the New England and Pacific regions (and for that matter, every other region of the country) increases in cohort headship over the 1950–1975 period far outstripped increases in the proportion of time spent outside marriage, particularly among women over 35 years of age. Thus headship and not marital changes accounted for most of the trend toward independent living of women through 1975, a conclusion we expect 1980 Census data to confirm.

The fact that the Pacific region, so heavily composed of recent migrants, leads the nation both in the proportion of women unmarried and in the household headship levels of unmarried women suggests one hypothesis to explain the headship trend: Alternatives to independent living, which for unmarried women have traditionally involved doubling up with close relatives, are fewer in areas of high immigration. Also, during the 1950–1975 period, opportunities for adults in the United States to share living quarters with a sibling declined generally, because the smaller families formed during the 1920s and 1930s yielded fewer living brothers or sisters for adults to live with 20 to 30 years later. Many of those who moved out west during the 1950s and 1960s were relatively "free" of family ties to begin with, and for migrants with close relatives, distance became an obstacle to close family ties and corresponding living arrangements.

The dramatic increase in independent living in the post–World War II period has maintained a constant pressure on the housing stock. This has in turn stimulated innovation in the housing market, making it possible for attached townhouses, mobile homes (the new term is "manufactured housing"), and condominiums to account for a significant and growing share of owned homes.

Perhaps the most salutary effect of the rise in household headship has been felt in older metropolitan areas, where more people living independently have cushioned the effects of declining growth in population in several ways. In slum areas the greater demand for housing has prevented the housing stock from being abandoned and from deteriorating as rapidly as might otherwise have occurred, and in some areas it has turned the deterioration process completely around. In more middle-class areas of cities— where young singles, divorced adults, and the better-off among the widowed congregate—high levels of labor-force participation, inflated property values, and burgeoning retail trade have all helped to ease the impact of population decline on city treasuries. In many vigorous cities, such as Boston, Philadelphia, Washington, San Francisco, and Denver, decline or deceleration cannot be seen with the naked eye.

Before the Census Bureau began to make estimates of intercensal population change in such cities, it was generally believed by city boosters that the decline documented in the previous census had "turned around," and the demographer's news that decline was continuing has generally been met with resistance and disbelief. With housing vacancy rates shrinking to under 2 percent, public transportation more overburdened, traffic problems getting worse, retail stores fighting for space, and all forms of public services being strained to the limits, how could population be declining? The one place where decline was all too evident was in the schools, and that provides the clue to the primary reasons for the net loss of population: low fertility and the flight of couples with school-age children to the suburbs. The replacement of households headed by married couples with children by childless couples and unmarried individuals has had a profound effect on neighborhoods, which no longer need to be organized around schools and the needs of children. At one very basic level, streets, houses, and apartments are empty for substantial parts of the day while neighborhood residents are at work. This increases vulnerability to burglary, causing people to suspect strangers and to protect their privacy. At another level, neighborhood change has undermined old political alliances and made room for newer, more progressive ideas concerning the relationships between a city and its residents.

Increasing levels of independent living among the unattached population have buffered the impact of population decline at some levels and accelerated changes at other levels, but further increases in headship rates have their limits. Unattached individuals probably never will achieve the almost universal household headship levels of married couples; we can expect upper limits to be reached when perhaps 70 to 80 percent of single, divorced, and widowed adults are living alone. In many areas these limits are being approached. When they are, a new urban neighborhood dynamic will take over. This new dynamic could mean more stability, but it also could mean a greater opportunity for neighborhood change if foreign immigrants continue to fill the void created by a native labor force that is failing to reproduce itself.

The Changing Racial and Ethnic Mix of Central Cities

One of the more pervasive demographic changes in store for the 1980s is the continued decline in the fraction of the United States population that is native born and white. This trend is well established in large cities, but recent demographic dynamics are changing the racial and ethnic structure of suburban communities as well. Decline in the relative size of the native white population at the national level stems from two factors: the above-average rates of natural increase among nonwhites and persons of hispanic origin,[7] and the large portion of the stream of foreign migrants that is hispanic. At the subnational level the pattern of internal migration, particularly the disproportionally white movement to exurban areas that emerged in the 1970s, has accelerated the shift toward greater concentrations of nonwhites and hispanics in metropolitan areas.

Over the 1970s a gradual shift took place in the composition of the minority population: the hispanic fraction increased. This shift was partly due to the decline in black fertility which closely paralleled the decline in white fertility. At the same time the fertility of hispanic persons remained at higher levels. More fundamentally, however, the black exodus from the rural South to the urban North has ended and perhaps reversed. Therefore, population redistribution no longer fuels expansion of the black urban population in the older northeastern metropolitan areas. Toward the end of the decade blacks moved from central cities into the suburbs at an ever greater pace, diminishing the impact of white migration out of the urban cores. In addition, hispanics have helped ease the pace of urban population decline in those areas losing population, both through immigration from abroad and through natural increase, and have also speeded growth in other metropolitan areas where total population is increasing. Nevertheless, since whites are still moving out of cities more rapidly than blacks, the gradual process of racial turnover has moved forward in the 1970s and will continue in the 1980s.

Precise measurement of these demographic trends is almost

Table 3.5   Changing Racial and Ethnic Mix over 1970s Decade of Central City Population of Incorporated Places 50,000 + with More than 10 Percent Nonwhite in 1980

Region	Number of Cities Included	Percent of All Cities 50,000+ in 1980	Total 1980 Population Included	Percent of Region's 1980 Population Included	Average of 1980 Populations		Mean Percent Change 1970–1980		
					% Nonwhite	% Spanish Origin	Total Population	% Nonwhite	% Spanish Origin
New England	14	37.8	1,944,649	15.8	21.9	8.7	−7.1	9.3	5.2
East North Central	45	53.6	11,081,762	26.6	26.7	3.9	−6.2	9.2	1.1
West North Central	9	34.6	2,259,547	13.2	20.7	2.6	−9.1	5.2	*
Mid-Atlantic	26	74.3	12,038,973	32.7	35.1	12.5	−9.5	13.8	6.7
South Atlantic	40	81.6	7,047,682	19.1	36.5	3.5	5.6	6.3	*
East South Central	13	92.9	3,040,900	20.7	38.7	0.8	16.8	4.8	*
West South Central	36	83.7	8,630,884	36.4	27.6	14.6	16.8	9.6	3.7
Mountain	10	37.0	2,786,122	24.5	15.8	16.7	27.9	9.9	4.3
Pacific (except Alaska and Hawaii)	65	73.0	12,361,288	38.9	23.2	18.8	11.4	15.1	7.9

* Less than 1 percent.
SOURCES: 1980 Census *Advance Reports* by State, Table 2; 1970 Census, *Characteristics of the Population*, state volumes, Tables 23, 81.

impossible because data on race and ethnicity are methodologically weak. The weaknesses include serious undercounts of the black population, a lack of strict comparability over time because of differences in questions about ethnicity, differences in the lists of examples included in questions on Spanish origin, ambiguity in the implied definitions of white and nonwhite, and differences in the definition of geographic units in which the data are organized. These are all serious obstacles to the investigation of trends and differentials in ethnic composition. The problem of undocumented aliens further complicates measurement. Thus we can only approximate "true" trends.

The last methodological weakness we listed, changing geographic definitions, can be corrected by reaggregating data so that boundaries are constant over time. However, the 1980 Census tables needed for such *post hoc* adjustment are not yet available to the public. Without holding boundaries constant, the proportion of a metropolitan area that is nonwhite may appear to decline between two censuses. If new suburban territory is added to the metropolitan area over the same period, the explanation on the shift in racial composition may simply be that the newly annexed areas are mostly white.

In order to get an indication of shifts in racial composition untainted by incomparable geographic areas, we have chosen to focus on the central cities of larger urban areas. Boundary changes for central cities are now rare. Table 3.5 presents data on the changing ethnic mix between 1970 and 1980 for incorporated places of 50,000 or more residents which were more than 10 percent nonwhite in 1980. There are 258 such cities, distributed across the nine Census regions as the first column indicates. This is 63 percent of all cities with over 50,000 inhabitants; the corresponding percentages for regions are in the second column. For convenience we will refer to these cities (population of at least 50,000, over 10 percent nonwhite) as "racially diverse cities" in the remainder of this chapter.

The first two columns of Table 3.5 show that the nonwhite population in the New England, West North Central, and Mountain regions is concentrated in relatively few cities. In the southern regions and Mid-Atlantic, the majority of large cities are racially diverse. Even in the regions where nonwhites are dispersed among most large cities, however, racially diverse cities account for a striking minority of the regions' total population. The third column in Table 3.5 provides the relevant data. In the Pacific region 38.9 percent of all people live in racially diverse cities, a larger fraction than do so in any other region. In the West North Central region 13.2 percent of the population lives in racially diverse cities, the smallest fraction among the regions.

The fourth and fifth columns of Table 3.5 give the average percentage nonwhite and percentage hispanic (with cities given equal weight) in 1980 for the racially diverse cities in the nine regions. Since cities with small nonwhite percentages are excluded from the table, it perhaps is not surprising that nonwhite fractions vary less than hispanic fractions. However, the concentration of hispanics—in certain parts of the country, in particular states within regions, and in particular cities within states—is more than a statistical artifact: Spanish language and culture can more easily thrive in places where there is a critical mass.

In the South Atlantic region few hispanics are found outside of Florida and Washington, D.C. Within Florida 16 cities have 50,000 or more inhabitants and 10 of these are racially diverse. But only two Florida cities included in Table 3.5, Miami and Tampa, contain concentrations of hispanics exceeding 10 percent of the total population, 56 percent and 13 percent respectively. One other large city, Hialeah, has an even larger concentration of hispanics, 75 percent; it is not included in Table 3.5 because its 1980 nonwhite population was just under 10 percent.

The Pacific region also has a majority of the hispanic population concentrated in one state, California. Within California, however, the hispanic population is much more dispersed than it is in Florida. Of the 81 cities of 50,000 or more people in California, 62 are racially diverse. The population in 53 of these 62 cities (the remaining three racially diverse Pacific cities are outside California) is more than 10 percent hispanic (mostly of Mexican origin). The pervasiveness of the hispanic population in California, with its above-average rates of natural increase, is another of the factors leading us to project that Pacific will grow faster than South Atlantic through the 1980s.

Three other regions contain states with concentrations of hispanics: Mid-Atlantic, Mountain, and West South Central. The states in question show less dispersion than California but significantly more dispersion than Florida. In the Mid-Atlantic region New York City and the eight racially diverse New Jersey cities (there are thirteen New Jersey cities with 50,000 or more inhabitants) are the places where hispanics have settled. In the West South Central states, Texas is the area of concentration for hispanics, with the great majority of the 23 racially diverse Texas cities having large concentrations of hispanic population. Here, as in Pacific, we project high growth for the 1980s, partly because of the higher than average natural increase expected from a relatively young and highly fertile hispanic population.

The Mountain region, while having a sizable hispanic population, is second only to West North Central in having the lowest concentration of nonwhites in its large cities. Only 10 percent of the 27 large cities in the Mountain region are racially diverse. In practically each Mountain state where there is a significant nonwhite population, there is a "primary" city where nonwhites are concentrated. Montana, Idaho, and Wyoming have no cities that are racially diverse by the criteria used in Table 3.5. In Colorado, New Mexico, and Nevada the "primary" nonwhite cities are Denver, Albuquerque, and Las Vegas. Utah and Arizona have two "primary" cities each with concentrations of nonwhites: Ogden, Salt Lake City, Phoenix, and Tucson. In Utah the increase in the urban nonwhite population has been accompanied by white flight into the suburbs of Ogden and Salt Lake City, resulting in a net loss of population over the 1970s of more than 7 percent in each city. In Arizona, as the proportion nonwhite in Phoenix and Tucson grew between 10 to 15 percent over the 1970s, total population in these cities grew 25 to 30 percent, indicating a very high rate of migration of nonwhites into these cities.

The last three columns of Table 3.5 show that in all regions of the country, whether racially diverse cities grew or shrank through the 1970s, the nonwhite fraction of the population increased and the hispanic fraction usually did also. In declining cities the increase in minority fractions was partly due to whites moving out of central cities and partly due to immigration of blacks and hispanics. The immigrants probably sought to take advantage of the jobs and housing opportunities that the emigrating whites abandoned; they often found jobs had left with the whites. In the growing cities, expanding job and housing opportunities attracted both native whites and other racial and ethnic groups. The high overall growth rates of the large cities in the bottom four regions in Table 3.5 demonstrate the powerful effect reinforcing migration of all racial and ethnic groups can have.

We have focused on the changing racial and ethnic mix of large cities in each region, and have not said much about suburban areas and small towns. To date, it appears that in the 1980s housing stocks, schools, and neighborhood environments will bring racial and ethnic changes to suburban areas, much as these features first attracted whites from urban cores. As the original suburbanites age well into the empty nest stage of their life cycle, some will move to smaller quarters; eventually all will die. Their houses will be bought by the next in line, and those next in line are increasingly black and hispanic. Evidence of large scale black and hispanic suburbanization, for example in the Chicago area, provides an indication of this trend for the future. There is, however, little evidence that a similar trend will affect exurban or rural areas in the 1980s.

These changes in suburban racial and ethnic mix seem, from our vantage point, inevitable in the long run. They will gain momentum in the 1980s. Not until the 1990s, however, will they become a major feature of our social and demographic landscape.

We have already summarized in Chapter 2 the joint effects of many demographic trends discussed in this chapter, and will not repeat this here. Instead, in Chapter 4 we turn to an analysis of detailed economic trends over the past several years.

Endnotes

1. See Calvin Beale, "The Revival of Population Growth in Nonmetropolitan America," ERS-Agriculture, June 1975; C. Beale and G. Fuguitt, "The New Pattern of Nonmetropolitan Population Change," Center for Demography and Ecology Working Paper 75-22, University of Wisconsin, 1975; Peter A. Morrison and Judith P. Wheeler, "Rural Renaissance in America?" *Population Bulletin* No. 31 (October 1976); Kevin McCarthy and Peter Morrison, "Post-1970 Demographic Change in Nonmetropolitan Areas: Insights from the 10-Percent CWHS," in U.S. Department of HEW, Policy Analysis with Social Security Research File (Washington: USGPO, 1978), pp. 635–660.

2. Larry Long and Diana DeAre, "Migration to Nonmetropolitan Areas: Appraising the Trend and Reasons for Moving," *Special Demographic Analyses*, CDS 80-2, U.S. Bureau of the Census of November 1980.

3. Calvin Beale, "Rural and Small Town Population Change: 1970–1980." Economics and Statistics Service, U.S. Department of Agriculture, 1981 (E55-5-FES 1981).

4. For a further discussion of New England, see George Masnick, "Demographic Influences on the Labor Force in New England," *Proceedings of Conference on Manpower Policy Issues*, Harvard Business School, May 15, 1981.

5. The Census Bureau's estimated rate of divergence in fertility over the 1970s decade is somewhat exaggerated because of errors the Bureau made in its estimates of intercensal changes in regional base populations. The higher-than-expected numbers of births in the South and West are partly due to more reproductive-age population living in these areas than the Census estimated. Likewise, the declines in fertility in the North and East were exaggerated by the higher-than-expected loss of young adults from these regions.

   The Total Fertility Rate is computed as the sum of age-specific fertility rates in a given year. The age-specific rates are the number of births in a given year to women who are a given age, divided by the total number of women that age. The TFR is therefore interpreted as the expected number of births that a hypothetical woman would have if she passed through her reproductive ages bearing children at rates characteristic of *current* levels of childbearing at each age. The TFR is not a good measure of the actual fertility of a particular cohort over its lifetime, because current social and economic conditions could be influencing women of all ages to be either accelerating or postponing childbearing, thus inflating or deflating the TFR over its long term average value.

6. George Masnick and Mary Jo Bane, *The Nation's Families: 1960–1990* (Boston, Auburn House, 1980). See also George Masnick, "The Continuity of Births-Expectations Data with Historical Trends in Cohort Parity Distributions: Implications for Fertility in the 1980s," in Gerry Hendershot and Paul Placek (eds.), *Predicting Fertility* (Lexington, Mass., D.C. Heath and Co., 1981), pp. 169–184.

7. Persons of Spanish origin (which we call "hispanic" in the text) were identified in 1970 by a separate question on sample Census questionnaires. A person was classified as being of Spanish origin or descent if his or her entry for this question was Mexican, Puerto Rican, Cuban, Central or South American, or Spanish. In 1980, all respondents to the Census questionnaire were asked to indicate whether they were of Spanish origin and specify Mexican, Mexican-American, Chicano, Puerto Rican, Cuban, or other Spanish/Hispanic. Additional questions about Spanish ancestry were asked of a 15 percent sample of respondents in 1980. The broader 1980 definition is expected to identify more respondents as being of Spanish origin, but not enough to account for the changes we discuss below.

Chapter 4

ECONOMIC GROWTH: DETAILED TRENDS

Economic growth in the United States has always had different effects in different regions. During several distinct historical periods, population and economic activity have grown more rapidly in some regions than in others. The westward movement of population in the 1800s opened entire new areas of the country for development. Until this time, growth had been concentrated on the eastern seaboard. Rapid industrialization in the late 1800s and early 1900s brought large numbers of people to urban factories and changed northeastern and midwestern cities' economic basis from commerce to manufacturing. Growth was concentrated in these areas because of the availability of transportation, the existence of cheap energy, and the proximity of commercial capital and final goods' markets.

Population and industry have been growing rapidly in the South and West since World War II. Recently growth in these areas has accelerated while growth in the North has slowed. In direct contrast to the growth during the industrial revolution of the 1800s and the westward migration toward the end of that century, economic expansion since the mid-1960s in the South and West has come at the expense of the North. It is this change that has caused concern (and often alarm) in the northern areas of the country.

In this chapter we examine how regional economies have grown and changed over time. We consider two measures of economic growth, employment and income, focusing on the former. The first section analyzes regional differences in employment growth rates for various industries and the resulting changes in regions' industrial mixes. The second section examines regional differences

95

in income, assessing the effects of changes in earnings, labor-force participation, and non-wage income on total income.

Employment

The South and West have grown substantially more than the North since 1950. Table 4.1 shows that nonagricultural employment grew twice as fast in the South and West as it did in the North between 1950 and 1965. Between 1965 and 1970 growth rates in the North were 2 to 3 percent per year, while rates in the South and West were approximately 4 percent per year. Growth in the South and West slowed after 1970, though it was still significantly greater than in the North. The Mid-Atlantic region even experienced a slight decline in nonagricultural employment in the 1970s.

Table 4.2 presents similar but starker data on manufacturing employment. Manufacturing employment grew slightly in the East North Central region and not at all in the North between 1950 and 1970. Employment actually declined in the 1970s, quite substantially in the Mid-Atlantic region. In all other regions except Pacific, growth rates were high between 1965 and 1970 and declined substantially in the early 1970s. Growth in the Pacific, the most industrially mature region outside the North, grew very rapidly in the 1950s and early 1960s but slowed somewhat after 1965.

Table 4.1   Annual Percentage Change in Nonagricultural Employment[a]

Region	1950–1965	1965–1970	1970–1977[b]
New England	1.31	2.73	0.90
Mid-Atlantic	1.11	2.24	−0.15
East North Central	1.61	2.66	1.22
West North Central	1.88	3.18	2.23
South Atlantic	3.58	4.72	2.87
East South Central	2.94	3.62	3.13
West South Central	3.20	4.25	4.26
Mountain	4.68	4.51	5.26
Pacific	5.02	4.03	3.00

[a] Calculated from data in Bernard L. Weinstein and Robert E. Firestine, *Regional Growth and Decline in the United States* (New York: Praeger Publishers, 1978), pp. 13–14. They are simple averages, i.e. n-year percentage change divided by n.
[b] 1977 data are provisional.

Table 4.2 Annual Percentage Change in Manufacturing Employment[a]

Region	1950–1965	1965–1970	1970–1977[b]
New England	−0.04	−0.05	−0.82
Mid-Atlantic	0.02	−0.08	−2.16
East North Central	0.59	0.56	−0.58
West South Central	1.61	2.60	0.60
South Atlantic	2.64	2.98	0.47
East South Central	3.19	3.92	1.25
West South Central	3.28	5.13	2.49
Mountain	4.85	5.08	2.13
Pacific	4.65	1.93	0.99

[a] Calculated from data in Bernard L. Weinstein and Robert E. Firestine, *Regional Growth and Decline in the United States*. New York: Praeger Publishers, 1978. Pages 16–18. They are simple averages, i.e. n-year percentage change divided by n.
[b] 1977 data are provisional.

In order to forecast future changes, we need to understand more about the nature of past trends. Is it reasonable to expect the South to continue growing at a uniformly rapid rate? Will the North continue to lose manufacturing employment? One way to begin to answer these questions is to look at employment changes for specific industries. For example, if the South and West have been gaining employment in "growth" industries, then they are likely to be in a strong position in the future. Examining employment trends by industry will also allow us to see whether the regions are becoming more alike with respect to industry mix.

We rely for this analysis on data collected by the Bureau of Economic Analysis (BEA) in the U.S. Department of Commerce. The BEA has been collecting employment data by state and industry since 1967, compiling information from state unemployment-insurance records and other sources as necessary. Our analysis runs from 1967 to 1978. The overall economy changed substantially during those years, so we divided the span into three periods. Although employment grew during all three periods, by most economic measures the first was the healthiest. The second period ended with the 1973–1975 recession, and thus the overall performance of the economy was more sluggish between 1970 and 1974 than it had been between 1967 and 1970. The third period, which included the gradual recovery from the 1973–1975 recession, saw the economy become somewhat less sluggish than it had been between 1970 and 1974, but not as vigorous as it had been in the first period.

Table 4.3 Employment Growth in the United States by Industry, 1967–1978

Industry	1967[a] Employment	Percent Change 1967–1978	Annual Growth Rate[b]			
			1967–1978	1967–1970	1970–1974	1974–1978
Total Wage and Salary Employment	73,536.9	25.35	2.30	1.94	2.14	2.28
Agriculture	1,648.2	6.39	0.58	− 1.58	1.30	1.54
Mining	596.8	30.90	2.81	− 1.00	2.54	5.63
Construction	3,344.0	28.20	2.56	2.12	2.96	1.94
Manufacturing	19,354.3	5.99	0.54	− 0.17	0.60	1.01
Transportation	2,579.9	7.16	0.65	0.78	0.62	0.54
Communications	967.0	28.34	2.58	5.38	1.58	0.98
Public Utilities	646.0	19.56	1.78	2.32	1.92	0.95
Trade	13,862.0	41.76	3.80	3.38	3.02	3.71
Finance, Insurance, and Real Estate	3,282.0	45.80	4.16	4.38	3.94	2.83
Services	12,195.6	43.79	3.98	3.07	3.47	3.91
Government	15,061.0	20.14	1.83	2.31	1.83	1.17

[a] In thousands.
[b] These are simple averages, i.e. n-year growth divided by n. The 1967–1978 rate is not the average of the three other rates since the base years differ.

The Total Picture

Total employment[1] in the United States grew by 25.4 percent between 1967 and 1978, an annual growth rate of 2.3 percent. (We calculate annual growth rates as arithmetic averages rather than geometric means, which overstates annual rates' deviations from zero somewhat. The ranking of different industries' or regions' rates is accurate, however.) Table 4.3 shows employment in 1967 and annual growth rates between 1967 and 1978 for 11 broad industry groups.[2] Trade, services, and finance, insurance, and real estate experienced the largest increases in employment. (For simplicity we will henceforth refer to the last of these— finance, insurance, and real estate—as finance.) They each grew about 44 percent over the period, or approximately 4 percent per year. Mining, construction, and communications also grew faster than total employment, though they are relatively small sectors. Public utilities and government grew at a slightly slower rate than total employment. Employment in manufacturing increased by only 6 percent, and not all industries within the group experienced growth.[3] Agriculture and transportation also experienced minimal growth.

The annual growth rate of total employment increased slightly between 1967 and 1978 from 1.9 percent in the first three years to 2.3 percent in the last four. Two opposing trends contributed to this result. On the one hand, the annual growth rate of trade, services, and manufacturing increased. Wholesale and retail trade grew by 3.4 percent annually between 1967 and 1970 and by 3.7 percent annually between 1974 and 1978; services by 3.1 percent and 3.9 percent; and manufacturing by -0.2 percent and 1.0 percent. (Growth rates in agriculture and mining also increased, but since these sectors employed relatively few people, they had little impact on overall growth.) On the other hand, the growth in the other six industries slowed between 1967 and 1978.

Table 4.4 shows how these changes affected the overall industrial mix in the country. The largest changes were in services and trade, each of which increased its share of total employment by 2.5 percentage points. Finance was the only other sector to increase its share of employment. The percentage employed in manufacturing declined from 26.3 percent in 1967 to 22.3 percent

Table 4.4   United States Industrial Mix, 1967–1978

	Percent Employed			
Industry	1967	1970	1974	1978
Total Wage and Salary Employment	100.00	100.00	100.00	100.00
Agriculture	2.24	2.02	1.96	1.90
Mining	0.81	0.74	0.75	0.84
Construction	4.55	4.57	4.71	4.65
Manufacturing	26.32	24.74	23.33	22.25
Transportation	3.51	3.39	3.20	3.00
Communications	1.31	1.44	1.41	1.35
Public Utilities	0.88	0.88	0.88	0.84
Trade	18.85	19.62	20.25	21.32
Finance, Insurance, and Real Estate	4.46	4.77	5.09	5.19
Services	16.58	17.12	17.95	19.02
Government	20.48	20.69	20.46	19.63

in 1978. There were no other substantial changes in the industrial mix.

The Regional Picture

Our next question concerns whether all regions experienced similar growth patterns, a question we can best answer by using shift-share analysis.[4] Regional employment growth has three components: growth that reflects overall national growth (the "national" effect); growth that reflects differences between the national and regional industry mix and the interaction of these with industry-specific growth rates (the "mix" effect); and growth that reflects differences between regional and national growth rates for each specific industry (the "shift" effect). We estimate the third component and use it to characterize regions.

Consider, by way of example, employment in the East South Central, which grew between 1967 and 1978 by 30.8 percent or 4,243,820 jobs (Appendix Table C.20). Total employment in the United States grew by 25.4 percent between 1967 and 1978. If the East South Central region's employment reflected only a "national" effect, it would have grown by the same 25.4 percent. However, as Table 4.3 shows, national growth rates vary by sector, ranging from 6 percent for the 11 years in manufacturing to almost

46 percent for finance. An extreme (and hypothetical) region that devoted all its economic activity to manufacturing would have grown by 6 percent over these 11 years if its manufacturing employment grew at the same rate as the nation's. One that devoted all its efforts to finance would have grown by almost 46 percent. Therefore, regional employment growth depends on the industry mix in the region. If each industry in the East South Central region had grown at the corresponding national rate, then total employment in the region would have grown by 24.6 percent. (The calculation is as follows: Multiply the growth rate for each sector, from Table 4.3, by the proportion of 1967 East South Central employment that was in this sector, from Appendix Table C.19. Then add up the resulting figures.) The difference between this mix-adjusted growth rate prediction, 24.6 percent, and the simple prediction based on total national growth, 25.4 percent, is the "mix" effect. Thus employment in the East South Central states grew by $24.6 - 25.4 = -0.8$ percent (that is, it was 0.8 percent smaller) because of the specific industry mix in that region.

Nevertheless, employment grew in the East South Central region by 30.8 percent (Appendix Table C.20) over this period. This is $30.8 - 24.6 = 6.2$ percentage points (the "shift" effect) higher than one might expect on the basis of national growth patterns and the region's industry mix. This 11-year "shift rate" for the region as a whole reflects the cumulative sum of individual shifts (that is, deviations of actual changes in number of jobs from nation-based expectations) for each industry in the region and each year in the period.

We also calculate the shift rate for individual industries within a region. For example, manufacturing employment grew by 26.2 percent in the East South Central between 1967 and 1978. Nationally, manufacturing grew by 6.4 percent. The manufacturing shift effect for this region is $26.2 - 6.4 = 19.8$ percent, an annual rate of 1.8 percent over the 11-year period. Thus manufacturing employment grew in the East South Central faster than it did nationally. The total shift rate for a region (discussed above) is the weighted sum of these industry-specific shift rates, the weights being each industry's share of employment in the region during the base period.

Both the overall regional shift rate and the corresponding industry figures are of interest. The former give us a sense of the region's behavior; the latter give us a sense of the homogeneity

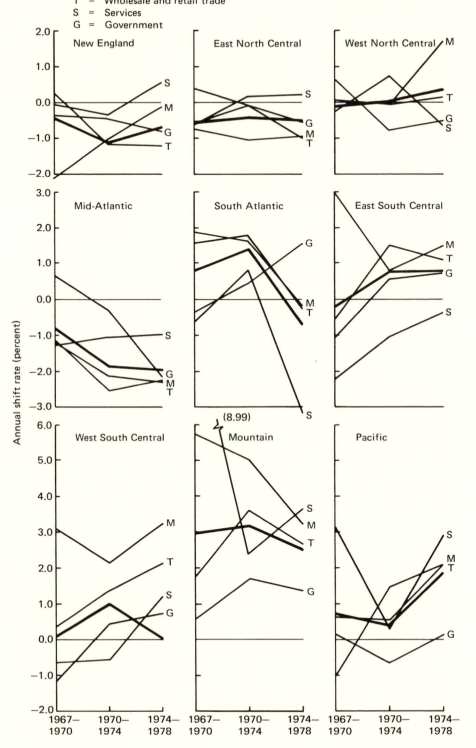

M = Manufacturing
T = Wholesale and retail trade
S = Services
G = Government

━━━ Total wage and salary employment

Annual shift rate (percent)

New England
East North Central
West North Central

Mid-Atlantic
South Atlantic
East South Central

West South Central
Mountain
(8.99)
Pacific

1967–
1970

1970–
1974

1974–
1978

of this behavior across industries and, where this is modest, of the offsetting gains and losses. We can repeat this exercise for subperiods between 1967 and 1978 and can translate period shift rates into annual shift rates. Appendix B delves further into the algebra of all this; suffice it to say here that these two "shift" effects—the deviation of regional growth rates by industry from national rates, and the deviation of aggregate regional growth rates from rates implied by the local mix and national rates—give us considerable insight into regional differences in economic growth.

Regions experienced substantially different growth patterns between 1967 and 1978. In general, the South and West grew much faster than the North. The shift rates for total employment and the four largest industries nationally—manufacturing, trade, services, and government—are plotted in Figure 4.1 for the nine regions. (Tables of shift rates, actual employment growth, and 1967 base employment are in Appendix Tables C.9–C.26.) These four industries represent 77 to 87 percent of total employment in these regions.

An industry that grew consistently at the national rate would be plotted as a horizontal line at zero (for example, trade in the West North Central). If an industry grew at a rate greater than the national average, the line would be above zero. The line is below zero for below-average growth. (Note that a negative shift rate does not indicate that the industry *actually* lost employment, because the shift rate tells us only where the region stood *relative* to the national average.) The striking feature of Figure 4.1 is that the different industry lines for a region tend to resemble each other. This indicates that within a region, industries exhibit similar growth patterns—that is, regional effects extend across industries. Shift-share analysis of still earlier periods has yielded similar results.

In Chapter 2 we projected slightly different growth for the New England and West North Central regions than we did for the Mid-Atlantic and East North Central regions. Much of this had to do with demographic trends, but there are preliminary indications of the distinction in Figure 4.1. Growth rates in the Mid-Atlantic were below average in every period and every industry (except government in the first period); they also tended to decline, relative to the average, over time. Growth in the East North Central

---

Figure 4.1   Shift Rates by Region and Larger Industry Groups, 1967–1978.

was also generally below average. The rates tended to increase a bit in the early 1970s, but they were constant after that. In contrast, growth in the New England and the West North Central regions appears to have picked up. In the West North Central, growth rates were about average between 1967 and 1974. However, after 1974 the growth rates in most industries, particularly in manufacturing, were above average. Growth rates in New England were generally below average during the entire period. However, the trend over time showed some improvement, particularly in manufacturing.

The southern and western regions are in quite different stages of development. For the most part they are all growing faster than average, as Figure 4.1 shows. The East South Central, West South Central, and Mountain regions, the smallest and least industrial ones, are growing most rapidly. The South Atlantic region grew strongly until 1974, when growth rates in all industries fell sharply. This is consistent with the demographic trends we observed in Chapter 3 and our projections in Chapter 2.

Employment in the Pacific region did not grow consistently over the time period. Growth rates fell dramatically during the second period, which led into the recession in 1973–1975, and then picked up remarkably in 1974–1978, suggesting that the region is sensitive to national economic conditions. Although no recent deceleration is evident for employment, a sluggish national economy is more likely to produce one here than it is in the Mountain or South Central regions. This is one reason why our projections for the Pacific carry a larger potential error than those for other regions.

The tables in Appendix C give the actual distribution of employment across industries for each region in 1967, 1970, 1974, and 1978. These distributions change either as the national distribution changes (Table 4.4 above) or as regional industry growth rates depart from national ones—that is, as shift rates depart from zero. The changes resulting from these two trends have varied from region to region, and we will discuss each briefly before moving on to our analysis of income.

Historically *New England* has been highly industrialized. In 1967 manufacturing employed one third of the work force. Only the East North Central employed a larger proportion in this sector. The loss of manufacturing employment between 1967 and 1974 and the slow growth between 1974 and 1978 reduced manufacturing employment to 27 percent of the total work force, a decline of almost six percentage points. However, New England remained one of the most industrialized regions. The fraction employed in construction also declined, reflecting the region's slow growth.

The fraction of New England's work force employed in services increased from 17.5 percent to 22.0 percent between 1967 and 1978. For trade the increase was from 18.4 percent to 20.9 percent. These two increases balanced losses in manufacturing. New England employed a higher percentage than any other region in services in 1978, having already been among the highest in 1967. The percentage of New England's work force employed in trade remained in the bottom third among regions. Government has always been a smaller employer in New England (and the entire North) than elsewhere in the country. The proportion employed in the sector fluctuated only slightly over time.

The industrial mix in *Mid-Atlantic* generally has resembled that of New England. The region employed a substantial fraction of its labor force in manufacturing (30 percent) and services (18 percent) in 1967. Government employed 16 percent, a relatively small amount, and the fraction employed in trade was also slightly less than average.

The changes in the Mid-Atlantic between 1967 and 1978 resembled the changes in New England. Manufacturing declined most in relative importance, to 24 percent of total employment in 1978. However, like New England, the Mid-Atlantic remained one of the most industrialized regions. Service and trade employment increased substantially, so that by 1978 the Mid-Atlantic employed almost as many service workers as manufacturing workers. The fraction of the work force employed in government remained stable over time, the fraction employed in transportation and construction dropped somewhat, and the fraction employed in finance and trade rose.

East North Central employed 34.6 percent of its work force in manufacturing in 1967, the highest percentage of all the regions. The region also employed a slightly higher fraction in transportation than New England or Mid-Atlantic did. The East North Central region had a smaller percentage in services than these other industrialized regions, but in all other respects the industrial mixes of the three areas were similar.

Manufacturing employment in East North Central declined to 29.5 percent of total employment by 1978, a drop of five per-

centage points. Despite this large decline—which resulted from
both national and shift effects—the region's concentration in manufacturing was larger than that of any other region. The fraction
employed in services increased more than three percentage points
from 14.7 percent in 1967 to 17.9 percent in 1978. However, the
region remained one of the lowest proportional employers of service workers. The fraction employed in the trade sector increased
two percentage points, as it did in the other regions. The government sector remained relatively small throughout the entire
period.

That the industrial mix in *West North Central* is substantially
different from those of the New England, Mid-Atlantic, and East
North Central regions is a fact to which anyone who has ever
crossed the northern Mississippi River can attest. In 1967 West
North Central employed only 22 percent of its work force in
manufacturing, compared with around 30 percent in the industrial
heartland. The fraction employed in manufacturing declined less
between 1967 and 1978 in West North Central than in these other
northern regions, a trend that partly reflects its positive shift rate.
West North Central also employed a slightly smaller fraction in
services than New England and Mid-Atlantic did in 1967. This
gap widened to three percentage points between 1967 and 1978,
in part because the West North Central shift rate dropped below
zero. The West North Central employed a larger fraction in trade
than any other region, 21 percent in 1967, and a larger fraction
in government and agriculture than the New England, Mid-Atlantic, and East North Central regions. These disparities still existed in 1978.

Employment in West North Central grew at about the national
average between 1967 and 1974. In this respect it was similar to
(if not slightly better off than) the other northern regions. However, its industrial mix was unlike those in the other northern
regions. Why, then, did the four regions experience similar growth
patterns? One explanation is that employment growth between
1967 and 1974 was slow for different reasons in these regions. The
New England, Mid-Atlantic, and East North Central regions may
have grown slowly because relative demand for the regions' products, particularly durables and construction, declined. The West
North Central region, on the other hand, may have grown slowly
because emigration of young adults constrained the supply of
labor.

There is some empirical support for this hypothesis. Chapter 3 shows that population in the West North Central declined by 3.9 percent in the 1960s because of emigration (and rose by 9.9 percent because of natural increase, for a net gain of 6 percent, consisting substantially of children and long-lived adults). New England experienced immigration during the same period while migration was insignificant in the Mid-Atlantic and East North Central regions. In addition, unemployment rates were lower in the two North Central regions than in New England and Mid-Atlantic between 1967 and 1973.[5] This is what one would expect if emigration sapped labor supply in the North Central regions while labor demand declined in New England and Mid-Atlantic.

Employment growth picked up in the West North Central (though not in the other three regions we are comparing) between 1974 and 1978. What caused the growth patterns to diverge? Chapter 3 shows that net emigration in the West North Central slowed to 0.7 percent during the 1970s. If this increased labor supply, it might partially explain why employment expanded. During this period the Mid-Atlantic and East North Central regions lost population because of migration. Immigration dropped to zero in New England. These trends could retard employment growth. If relative demand for these regions' products continued to decline, employment would slow even more.

South Atlantic, Pacific, and East South Central are the most industrially mature regions in the South and West. Population and employment expanded in these three regions before they did in the Mountain and West South Central regions. The South Atlantic employed 22 percent of its work force in manufacturing in 1967, roughly the same proportion as the Pacific and East South Central regions did but much greater than the corresponding 12 percent in Mountain and 17 percent in West South Central. All southern and western regions employed a much higher fraction of their work forces in government than the northern regions did. The South Atlantic's fraction was the largest, 25 percent by 1978. But the South has proportionally less service employment than the North or West. South Atlantic's service fraction was 16.7 percent in 1978, the lowest of any region.

Since the South and West were gaining population and employment, construction accounted for a larger fraction of the labor force there than in the North. The South Atlantic employed about 5 percent of its labor force in construction. This was less than the very rapidly growing Mountain and West South Central regions but substantially more than the New England or Mid-Atlantic regions.

The industrial mix in the South Atlantic changed much less than that of any other region between 1967 and 1978. The fraction employed in manufacturing dropped by two percentage points between 1967 and 1978, to 20 percent. The government fraction dropped about one percentage point. In modest contrast, the trade fraction increased by three percentage points and the finance fraction by one percentage point.

The *East South Central* region is similar to South Atlantic, with two exceptions. First, East South Central had a larger fraction of its work force in manufacturing than any other southern or western region, just over 25 percent. The stability of this fraction between 1967 and 1978 partly reflected consistently positive shift rates. Second, although the East South Central employed a large fraction of its work force in government, the fraction was not quite as high as that in the South Atlantic.

This region employed an above-average fraction of workers in services in 1967. However, a steadily negative shift rate between 1967 and 1978 made the 1978 service fraction one of the lowest in the country. (The South Atlantic was the only other region to experience a decrease in the service fraction of employment.) The construction fraction, in contrast, was relatively high, though not quite as high as those of the more rapidly growing Mountain and West South Central regions. Trade in the East South Central, as in the South Atlantic, employed a smaller fraction of the labor force than it did in other regions. In fact, the East South Central had the lowest trade fraction in the country in both 1967 and 1978.

Despite the fact that the *West South Central* was one of the most rapidly growing regions, its manufacturing base was relatively low. Only 17 percent of the labor force worked in this sector in 1967, a substantially smaller proportion than in any other region except Mountain. Construction employment was high and increasing as a result of the region's extremely high growth rates. The fraction of the work force employed in construction was twice that of the North in 1978.

This region had a larger fraction of its work force employed in services in 1967 than any other region did. However, like that of East South Central, its service share did not increase between

1967 and 1978, despite a positive shift rate between 1974 and 1978. (This occurred because other industries grew even faster than services.) The West South Central was one of the lowest-ranked regions with respect to services fraction in 1978, in which respect it resembled the rest of the South.

The government was a large employer here in 1967 and remained so, even though the fraction employed in this sector decreased by over three percentage points by 1978. The region ranked in the top third of all regions with respect to its trade fraction, which increased about two percentage points during the study period.

Only 12 percent of the *Mountain* region's work force—the smallest in the nation—was employed in manufacturing in 1967. Despite tremendous employment growth and a positive shift rate, this fraction did not change at all between 1967 and 1978. The construction industry, on the other hand, increased its employment fraction from 5 percent in 1967 to 6.8 percent in 1978. The latter was the highest in the country, a clear indication of the relationship between *rates* of regional growth and *levels* of construction activity. The government employed 30 percent of the labor force in 1967 and 24 percent in 1978, a change due substantially to a decrease in military employment. The region's trade fraction ranked in the top one third of all regions. The Mountain region employed only 15 percent of its labor force in services in 1967, the lowest service fraction of any region. This rose to 19 percent in 1978, somewhat above the average.

The industrial mix in the Mountain region was quite similar to the mix in West South Central, the other rapidly growing region. Both had a relatively small manufacturing fractions and large trade, government, and construction fractions. These two regions also had substantial mining and agriculture. The major difference between the two regions was in services: Mountain had a relatively small service sector in 1967 but a relatively large one in 1978, and the opposite was true in West South Central.

The *Pacific* region resembles no other region in industry mix—as in other attributes. The region employed 21.5 percent of its work force in manufacturing in 1967 and 18 percent in 1978, with most of the decline occurring between 1967 and 1970. These fractions are similar to South Atlantic's and thus substantially smaller than those of New England and Mid-Atlantic, but they are larger than those of the rapidly growing Mountain region.

Pacific, like Mountain, employed a relatively low fraction in services in 1967; this increased substantially by 1978.

The Pacific region, like the rest of the South and West, had a large though declining fraction employed in government. Unlike the other fast-growing regions, however, its construction fraction was relatively low and, in fact, much more similar to the percentage found in the North than to those in the South and West. Limited construction in the face of increasing population leads to tight housing—another reason we distinguished Pacific from other historically fast-growing regions in Chapter 2.

Income

Increased income in a region signals economic growth. (Income includes wages and salaries from work and income from other sources.) If the increase exceeds inflation, the region's economic condition improves. If a region's total income, adjusted for inflation, increases relative to its population, individual well-being in the region increases.

Different regions of the country have very different per-capita income levels. This section examines these differences as they have changed over time. Conceptually, per-capita income is the product of five ratios: total income to total earnings, total earnings to total employees, total employees to total labor force, total labor force to total working-age population, and total working-age population to total population.

These five ratios have substantive meaning, of course. The ratio of income to earnings (which we will call the "income rate") tells us how dependent the regional economy is on labor income, which is closely determined by industrial activity, and how dependent it is on unearned income, which consists both of investment income and of transfer payments, such as welfare, unemployment payments, Social Security, and private pensions. The ratio of earnings to employment ("earnings rate") is a measure of regional wages which differs from simple wage rates in three respects: it measures annual rather than hourly wages, it includes proprietors' income as "earnings" and proprietors as "employees," and it does not adjust employee counts to full-time equivalents. (The last is important in the Mid-Atlantic region, as we will see below.) The earnings rate changes when industry wage rates change, when the industry mix changes, or when the prevalence of part-time work changes. The ratio of employment to labor force ("employment rate"), which is 1.0 (or 100 percent) less the unemployment rate, is an indication of the overall health of the regional economy. The ratio of the labor force to working-age population ("participation rate") is a measure of the potential availability of labor. It is safe to assume that the potential labor supply from current residents is less elastic in a region with a high labor-force participation rate than it is in one with a low rate. Finally, the ratio of working-age to total population ("availability rate") translates the region's age structure into a constraint on the labor force.

We argued in Chapter 2 that the somewhat counterintuitive growth patterns of the 1970s, in which both people (who are attracted by high per-capita income) and jobs (which are attracted, in part, by low earnings per employee) moved to the same regions, resulted from specific interactions among these ratios. The first issue, then, is concerned with how regional differences in the five ratios contribute to regional variations in per-capita income. The only consistent time-series data available do not include information on the number in the labor force or, for that matter, the size of the working-age population. Therefore we substitute for the last three ratios one approximate one, total employment divided by total population. We will call this variable the "working rate."

We present the component equation for each region for 1960, 1969, and 1978 in Table 4.5. From the table it is clear that variation in earnings per employee (W/E) dominates interregional variation in per-capita income. The working rate (employment/population, or E/P) plays some role, definitely more than the ratio of income to earnings. But in 1960, for example, the range in working rate relative to its mean was only about half as great as the range in earnings per employee relative to its mean. The same was true in 1969 and 1978. In all cases the East South Central region has the lowest per-capita income *and* the lowest earnings per employee *and* the lowest working rate. But another poor region, South Atlantic, did not have a low working rate (we commented on this in Chapter 2). A third relatively poor region, West South Central, had low participation rates in 1960 and 1969 but not in 1978. The ratio of income to earnings (T/W) is important for only one region, New England.

Table 4.5 Components of Per-Capita Income: Historical Trends

	1960				1969-II				1978			
Census Region	$\frac{Y}{W}$ ·	$\frac{W}{E}$ ·	$\frac{E}{N}$	= PCI	$\frac{Y}{W}$ ·	$\frac{W}{E}$ ·	$\frac{E}{N}$	= PCI	$\frac{Y}{W}$ ·	$\frac{W}{E}$ ·	$\frac{E}{N}$	= PCI
New England	1.256	6,746	.393	3,330	1.283	7,878	.447	4,513	1.351	8,198	.476	5,269
Mid-Atlantic	1.220	7,523	.385	3,531	1.240	8,703	.431	4,649	1.334	9,269	.441	5,455
East North Central	1.200	7,380	.369	3,272	1.201	8,616	.425	4,395	1.261	9,483	.458	5,478
West North Central	1.236	6,173	.369	2,812	1.233	7,246	.433	3,871	1.286	8,066	.489	5,071
South Atlantic	1.210	5,720	.365	2,523	1.220	7,127	.431	3,746	1.309	7,936	.470	4,879
East South Central	1.214	5,079	.332	2,050	1.218	6,527	.388	3,085	1.281	7,570	.436	4,227
West South Central	1.239	5,789	.347	2,488	1.245	6,982	.402	3,497	1.292	8,220	.460	4,882
Mountain	1.211	6,662	.352	2,840	1.232	7,356	.408	3,701	1.281	8,160	.478	5,001
Pacific	1.224	7,683	.380	3,569	1.224	8,801	.431	4,640	1.288	9,423	.484	5,876
U.S. Total	1.219	6,758	.369	3,039	1.228	7,955	.424	4,144	1.296	8,694	.464	5,227

SOURCE: Y/W = Personal Income/Earnings ratio, Appendix Table A.1 and related BEA data.
  W/E = Earnings per employee, from Appendix tables A.1 and A.4.
  E/N = Employment/Population ratio, from Appendix tables A.4 and A.7.

We now turn to an examination of the individual components of per-capita income.

Earnings

Regional data on wage and salary income per worker are plotted in Figure 4.2, based on the relevant columns in Table 4.5 (remember that these are constant 1972 dollars). As we noted above, these data change not only with wage rates but also with the level of self-employment, the industry mix, and the level of part-time employment. Regional differences in the first two of these extraneous influences did not change appreciably between 1960 and 1978, and thus the patterns in Figure 4.2 would be unchanged if we took them into account. The interregional differences in part-time employment apparently did change over this period, however, since taking full-time equivalency into account (as Lynn Browne has done elsewhere; see Appendix Table C.27) changes the Mid-Atlantic region's trajectory from one of convergence (Figure 4.2) to one of stability relative to the national average (Appendix Table C.27). The likely reason for this discrepancy between our data and those taking full-time equivalency into account is a steady decline in the number of hours the average Mid-Atlantic employee worked.

There was some convergence of regional earnings between 1960 and 1978. However, the convergence was due to relative changes in only four of the nine regions. Among the high-wage Pacific, East North Central, and Mid-Atlantic regions, only Pacific experienced a decline in relative wages and salaries, from 13.7 percent above average in 1960 to 8.4 percent above average in 1978. Neither East North Central nor Mid-Atlantic showed any significant change. (As we noted above, convergence for Mid-Atlantic reflects a decline in the average hours each employee worked.) The South Atlantic, East South Central, and West South Central regions had the lowest relative wages, 15 to 25 percent below average, in 1960. Wages rose fairly steadily after 1964 in these regions, and by 1978 each had increased its relative earnings by at least five percentage points. Wages in the Mountain region were roughly at the national average in the beginning of the period and dropped slightly by 1978. Both New England and West North Central had below-average wages throughout the entire period.

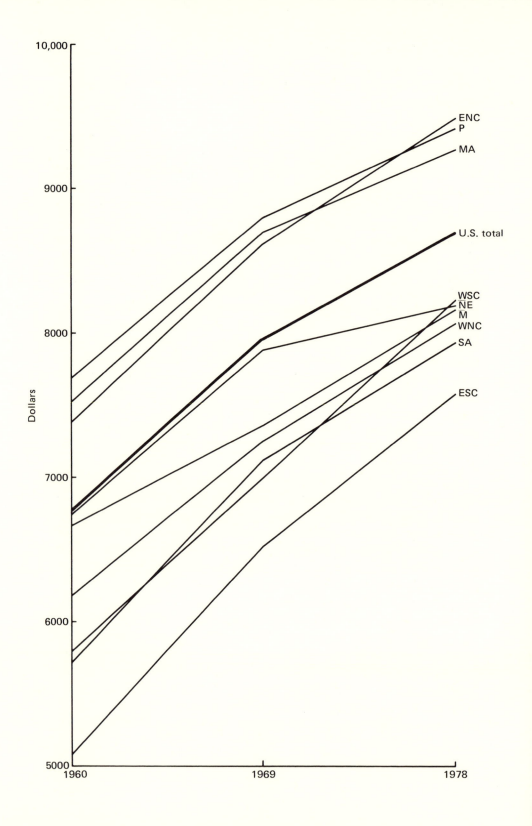

As we suggested in Chapter 2, there is no simple relationship among a region's employment growth, its relative wage, and the change in either of these variables. As we showed above, the four northern regions generally had below-average employment growth in the 1970s. (The one exception is West North Central, which grew faster than average during 1974–1978.) Two of these four regions, New England and West North Central, were low-wage regions, whereas Mid-Atlantic and East North Central had relatively high wages. Despite these disparities, relative earnings per employee did not change at all in three of these regions between 1960 and 1978, and the change in the fourth, Mid-Atlantic, is attributable to hours worked rather than to wage rates.

The South and West had rapid employment growth and (except for the Pacific region) relatively low wages. Pacific has always had the highest wages in the country, even after a relative decline over the period. Employment grew fastest in the Mountain and West South Central regions. Relative wages remained low, but those in West South Central improved somewhat. East South Central and South Atlantic both experienced increases in relative wages between 1960 and 1978, although they were still below average in 1978.

Working Rate

Figure 4.3 plots the data on working rates from Table 4.5 (with no adjustment for national trends). Working rates vary with the percentage of the population that is of working age, with the proportion of the working-age population that seeks work (this is the labor-force participation rate), and with the proportion of the work seekers who find work (the employment rate). Consistent series for these different ratios are hard to find, and in any case the interactions between employment rates and labor-force participation rates make separate analysis difficult. We present some sketchy data on labor-force participation in Appendix Table C.28, but concentrate here on the overall ratio of employees to total population.

The dominant trend in Figure 4.3 is the general increase in the working rate over the 1960–1978 period. Throughout these 19

Figure 4.2   Wage and Salary Earnings per Worker, 1960–1978 (1972 dollars).

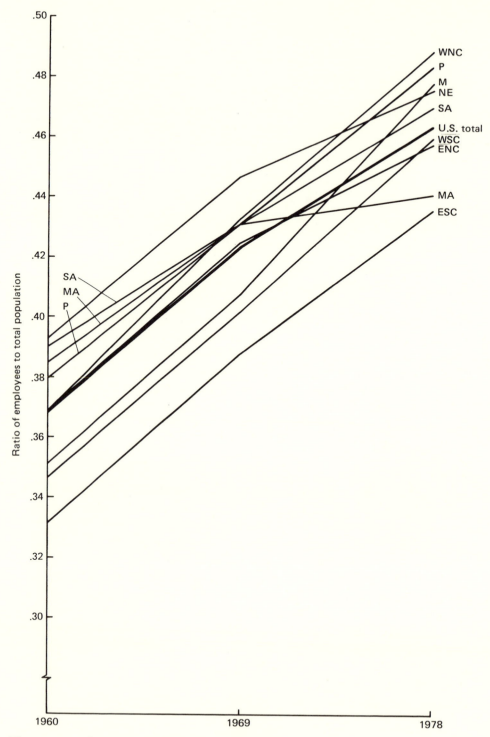

Figure 4.3   Labor-Force Participation, 1960–1978.

years the South Atlantic working rate grew more slowly than the national average. In the 1970s working rates in New England, Mid-Atlantic, and East North Central also grew more slowly than the national average (and, for that matter, more slowly than they had before). The leveling was substantial in Mid-Atlantic. At the same time, the working rate in Mountain rose more quickly than it did during the 1960s, moving this region from near the bottom to near the top of the distribution. Some of these shifts are attributable to the disproportionate movement of working-age and other populations from region to region; others reflect changes in labor-force participation such as those discussed in Chapter 2.

Non-Wage Income

Only New England and Mid-Atlantic benefited disproportionately from non-wage income, as Table 4.5 shows. Thus the variable had small effects on the distribution of per-capita income. This may well change when the baby boom reaches retirement age. These cohorts' distributions across regions may bring regions other than New England and Mid-Atlantic disproportionate shares of non-wage (primarily pension) income, and the variable's importance may increase commensurately.

Per-Capita Income

Figure 4.4 shows regional per-capita income for 1960, 1969, and 1978. There are substantial regional differences in all periods, which reflect differences in the underlying ratios.

The convergence since 1960 is evident. This trend is not new, however. Regional differences in per-capita incomes have been diminishing since the BEA began collecting data in 1929, and estimates for earlier years suggest the trend began before 1929. The regional ranking on per-capita income (Figure 4.4) is generally similar to the regional ranking on earnings per worker (Figure 4.2). The one exception is that New England ranks above average on per-capita income but below average on earnings per worker. This difference occurs because New England has a relatively high labor-force participation rate, and because property income is a more important source of income there than it is in other regions.

Comparing the trends in earnings per worker and per-capita income (Figures 4.2 and 4.4), we find that two differences are evident. First, the regional variation in per-capita income is much

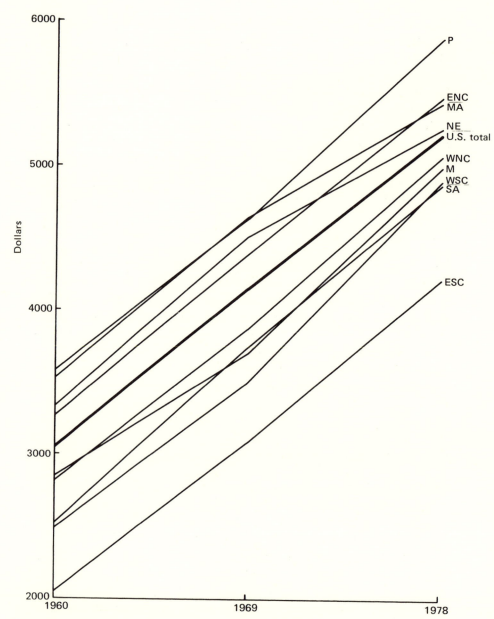

Figure 4.4   Per-Capita Income, 1960–1978 (1972 dollars).

greater than the variation in earnings per worker in 1960. Second, regional differences in per-capita income diminished much more than did differences in earnings per worker during the 1960s and 1970s.

Regional changes in the labor-force participation rate account for most of these differences. The South historically has had lower labor-force participation than the North, as Figure 4.3 shows. Changes in the rate over time have not been uniform, but overall the most recent periods have favored the South. Property income has been a more important source of income in the North, particularly New England and Mid-Atlantic, than in the South, with differences decreasing over time. Retirement income, another important source of non-wage income, is related to past earnings. Since earnings were historically higher in the North than in the South, so was retirement income. The increases in southern earnings over time have decreased differences in retirement income, as has the migration of retirees to the South. A final factor that has helped to reduce regional differences in non-wage per-capita income is the increase in government transfers (other than Social Security), which generally vary inversely with income. Thus equalization of non-wage income may have an increasing influence on per-capita income.

Endnotes

1. Total employment refers to total wage and salary employment. It excludes the self-employed.
2. We also examined a 37-category industrial grouping. The primary difference between the two groupings was that the 37-category group had much more detail in the manufacturing sectors than the 11 categories reported here. However, analysis of the 11- and 37-category groups gave similar results.
3. Industries that lost employment were food, textiles, apparel, primary metals, transportation equipment (except motor vehicles), and fabricated metals. Growing industries included paper, printing and publishing, chemicals, petroleum products, nonelectrical machinery, electrical equipment, motor vehicles, lumber, and other manufacturing.
4. Shift-share analysis has been criticized on a number of grounds; see Appendix B.
5. William Wheaton, "Metropolitan Growth, Unemployment, and Interregional Factor Mobility," in W. Wheaton (ed.), *Interregional Movements and Regional Growth*. Washington, D.C.: Urban Institute, 1979, pp. 248–249.

Chapter 5

REGIONAL ISSUES
IN THE 1980s

We have thus far highlighted two aspects of regional economic and demographic diversity: growth rates and levels. Together these lead to conclusions that regions are converging along some dimensions (those where high growth rates accompany low levels, as is true for per-capita income) while they are diverging along others (where high growth corresponds to high levels, as is true for school-age populations). Regional diversity in growth rates, which we have documented for the recent past and predicted for the proximate future, does not necessarily imply regional diversity on levels: The Mountain region's current population may be growing faster than New England's, for example, but the two regions' populations are not dissimilar. Nor do regional similarities on one dimension necessarily imply similarities on others: Although their total populations are similar, the population densities of the Mountain and New England regions are dramatically different.

To assess the implications of these convergences and divergences, we must also consider the substantive importance of regional differences compared with national levels and trends. In other words, are regional similarities (which can be summarized as national trends) or regional differences (which make national trends bad estimates of regional trends) more important? To pursue this question, we first consider several basic trends where regional differences are particularly important: fertility, migration, and the resulting age structure; and industry mix, labor-force participation, and the resulting wage and employment trends. This done, we address the question of limits to regional growth, turning finally to implications of the regional and national trends we have discussed for household patterns, urban life, working conditions, social services, and political balance.

Regional Trends

Fertility

Figure 3.4 plotted the ratios of regional total fertility rates to the national average from 1940 to 1977. An insert on that figure showed the national rate's oscillations for those years. In 1940, the year of maximum dispersion among regions, the minimum (Mid-Atlantic) and maximum (Mountain and East South Central) total fertility rates differed by 53 percent of the national average. This can be compared with variation in the national fertility rate, which between 1940 and 1980 ranged from 66 to 138 percent of its average value. Thus the national range is almost half again as large as the maximum interregional range and three times the minimum interregional range, which occurred around 1970.

Regional fertility trends thus depend heavily on national trends. These national trends are familiar by now. Birth rates jumped after World War II, reversing a long, slow decline. Rates resumed their decline after 1965 and leveled off somewhere in the mid-1970s. The resulting large cohorts born between 1945 and 1965 have moved gradually through the social system, causing a sequence of institutions to expand rapidly and then shrink.

There was considerable regional variation in fertility through the baby-boom years, with high rates in the Mountain and South Central regions balancing low rates in the Mid-Atlantic and New England regions. Toward the end of the period, fertility rates in the latter areas increased, while in the former they decreased. There were also more complex changes resulting, in part, from differences in age-specific fertility (total fertility broken down by age of mother). These regional differences caused children of the same cohort to be born over slightly different periods in different regions. These differences in age-specific fertility, which were plotted in Figure 3.5, will also influence future-period fertility patterns. Had baby-boom mothers grown up where they were born, their own children would have arrived earlier in the southern regions, which historically have had higher fertility below age 25, than in northern regions, which historically have had higher fertility above age 25. Instead of staying put, however, many baby-boom cohorts have relocated toward the South and West, as we saw in Figure 3.3. The children of these migrants will either expand the cohort size of the baby boomlet in their new regions, if the migrants adopt the fertility habits of the natives, or extend it over a longer period, if they retain the fertility patterns of their home regions. Limited evidence suggests the former, when-in-the-South-do-as-the-Southerners-do pattern.

In either case, the baby boomlet obviously will be more substantial in regions that have attracted young migrants than in those that have lost them. It is entirely possible that, because of migration and fertility patterns, there will be no discernible boomlet in the population of some regions (New England, Mid-Atlantic, and East North Central), a sharp one in others (East South Central and West South Central), and a substantial but smooth one in still others (Pacific and Mountain). For one region, South Atlantic, rapidly shifting fertility patterns make prediction difficult. The existence of the boom and boomlet cohorts is a national phenomenon, but their distribution across regions reflects substantial regional differences in fertility.

Migration

The migration of young adults to the South and West was only part of the migration pattern we described in Chapter 3. As fertility has declined, migration has accounted for an increasingly substantial part of regional population change. Here, by definition, regional differences are more important than national trends. The important general feature of regional migration is its age specificity, on which we commented in Chapter 3. Most migrants are either young adults entering the labor force or older adults retiring from the labor force.

We argued in Chapter 2 that different motivations underlie these two flows. Young adults respond to differences in employment or income prospects. Older ones respond to differences in lifestyle (which includes climate) and cost of living. The interaction of these tastes with regional attributes has drawn both sorts of migrants to southern and western regions for the past decade or two, with older migration directed southeast and young migration directed southwest. There are preliminary indications, which we discussed in Chapter 3, that these patterns are shifting slightly:

Both groups of migrants are distributing themselves more evenly across the South. In addition, migration patterns for the West North Central region are changing, apparently because the net loss of older migrants is ending.

Age Structure

The consequence of trends in fertility and migration shows in the age structure, and the combined effects of these two forces are to make national trends predict regional trends poorly. Three "bulges" are significant in the national population: people born before 1920, who are almost all out of the labor force by now; people born following World War II, who are finishing school, passing through their childbearing years, entering the housing market, and migrating; and the children of the baby-boom cohorts, who are of preschool age in some regions and just being conceived in others. The first bulge is in fact nothing of the kind. It appears large because the cohorts that followed were small, a result of low fertility in the Depression and of restrictions on foreign immigration in the 1920s and 1930s. Nevertheless, this first bulge was a national phenomenon, although small flows from many states to Florida have accentuated it in this state. The second bulge, the postwar baby boom, was also a national phenomenon, but this is changing as the cohorts redistribute themselves across the regions. The third bulge, a direct product of the second, will vary from region to region, according to the location and fertility of the baby-boom cohorts.

These three bulges affect regional development in two ways. First, the differences between their size and that of adjacent, nonbulge cohorts cause swings in school-age and college-age populations, housing demand, pension-fund outlays, and other social parameters where rapid cyclic change is difficult to manage. Second, the relative size of different bulges creates difficult political choices, such as the choice between reasonable Social Security taxes for young workers and reasonable benefits for retired ones.

Industrial Mix

As we showed in Chapter 4, different regions devote different portions of their economic structure to different industries, and these distributions have changed over time. There is little evidence that regional industry mixes are converging to a national norm (except, perhaps, in manufacturing), and on substantive grounds there is little reason to expect such convergence. Regional differences are important, in the sense that they are stable, but the national industry mix is the dominant influence.

There is some reason to expect regional differences in industry mix, however modest, to have predictable effects on regional development. That is, regions heavily invested in slow-growth industries should experience slower growth than those invested in high-growth industries. However, our shift-share analysis in Chapter 4 suggested this was not so. Regions' employment growth depended far less on industry mix than it did on intra-industry differences between regions. In other words, although trends in the national industry mix and in national growth within industries affected regional employment growth, they accounted for only a small fraction of actual changes in regional employment, because fast-growing regions grew rapidly and slow-growing regions grew slowly in most employment sectors.

Labor-Force Participation

The percentage of the national population that was working or seeking work rose from just under 60 percent in 1960 to over 63 percent in 1978, in large part because women entered the labor force in increasing numbers. Regional trends were somewhat more complex, since participation rates depended on changes in both the number of participants and the number of nonparticipants. In some regions, especially Mid-Atlantic, the emigration of young workers decreased participation rates, even though the young adults who stayed behind did not change their labor-force behavior. In South Central regions, on the other hand, the arrival of these young adults had the opposite effect. It is thus difficult to make unambiguous statements about national and regional trends in labor-force participation. But national effects, such as those discussed in the earlier Joint Center volume, *The Nation's Families: 1960–1990*, clearly have a substantial effect.

Wages and Employment

The regions least heavily invested in slow-growth industries have also been those with the lowest labor-force participation rates and the lowest wages. These regions suffered less than others as the economy slowed in the 1970s, leading to a widespread (and accurate) perception that living standards were improving faster in these regions. The combination of historically low labor-force participation, low wages, and appealing living conditions made it possible for the economies of regions to grow rapidly, attracting both migrants and jobs without changing the appeal of the regions. There is limited evidence that this cycle is ending in South Atlantic and even more limited evidence that it is starting up in West North Central. Employment shifts are a clear example of regional differentiation, which depends both on specific regional attributes (in this case low wages and elastic labor supplies) and on national tastes (of individuals for improved living standards and of business for low labor costs). As either of these changes, so will regional diversity in employment patterns.

Regional Effects

How does all this work out over the next few years or decades? There are several answers to this question, one of which we have already given: Regions grow disproportionately, and regional diversity increases. But regions cannot grow indefinitely; eventually limits operate. These may vary from region to region, as they do from nation to nation.

Until now, we have written little about resources, the major factor limiting growth. A complete catalog of regional resources in the United States is beyond the scope of this volume, but we can sketch its dimensions, using a framework proposed for international analysis by Richard J. Barnet in *The Lean Years*.

Barnet frames his analysis with an inventory of five critical resource systems: energy, nonfuel minerals, food, water, and human skills. In relatively few cases, he points out, do areas of the world balance their demand for these resources with the requisite supplies. Instead, most regions either import what they need from other regions or export their oversupply to regions that need it. By analogy with a modern factory, Barnet sees areas becoming highly specialized, each contributing its resources to global production organized by major nations and multinational companies. The keys to this scenario are two: Resources must remain concentrated, so that they may be used efficiently; and the whole

system must be managed. Globally, Barnet sees national rival-
ries—the "lifeboat" phenomenon—ensuring the former and multinational companies the latter. If we were to draw from Barnet's
work a prediction for the regions of the United States, it would
be that a strong national government would organize production
around regional resources without attempting to change the resource endowments of specific regions.

We can reserve discussion of government strength to the conclusion of the chapter and consider briefly each of the resources
Barnet lists. Energy, in the United States, comes from petroleum,
coal, nuclear fuels, water-driven turbines, and several minor
sources. These are regionally concentrated. Fossil fuels are found
primarily in the West South Central, West North Central, and
Mountain regions and hydraulic power in the Pacific and Mountain
regions. Although uranium deposits are also concentrated, the low
ratio of transportation costs to energy value for this fuel and the
potential for fuel recycling or breeding make the concentration
of uranium deposits unimportant. Minerals are heavily concentrated in the Mountain region. Food comes primarily from the
North Central, South Atlantic, East South Central, and Pacific
regions. Water is available in each region, but the match between
supply and demand is unfavorable in the Mountain, Pacific, and
West South Central regions. Human skills, which we might
equally well call labor supply, is distributed across the regions,
though prices (wages) differ. As with the other resources in the
United States, the supply of human skills tends to flow across
regional boundaries in response to economic forces.

This interregional sharing of resources differentiates the United
States from aggregations of autonomous nations and thus reduces
the applicability of Barnet's analysis to the United States. Regions
in the United States have not remained specialized resource pro-
viders, and resource sharing has kept any region from reaching
limits to its growth. In other words, regions have developed differently not because the fast-growth regions have been less limited
than the slow-growth regions but because the forces we outlined
in Chapter 2 favored them.

Nevertheless, there are potential limits to regional growth, and
these affect different regions differently. Perceived limits thus may
increase regional diversity, even though real limits are inconse-
quential. We have already alluded to one such limit, water supplies in the Pacific and Mountain regions. Another limit, energy

supplies, causes northern energy costs to exceed southern or western ones. But this effect should diminish as artificial ceilings on domestic energy prices, which have kept southern and western energy costs low, vanish. (The rapidly decreasing ratio of transportation to fuel extraction or importation costs has a similar effect.) A third limit, inadequate response of housing supply to housing demand, is widely believed to influence Pacific growth, but the modest slowdown we see in this region offers skimpy support for this argument. Limits, in short, will have some effects, but they will not be an important determinant of regional diversity in the 1980s.

What, then, are the net implications of the regional economic and demographic trends we have projected? We foresee impacts in five areas: household structure, working conditions, urban life, social services, and politics.

Household Structure

When young or retired adults leave one region for another, they destabilize housing demand. Consider, as a benchmark, the uncomplicated process. Young adults live with parents until they marry and can afford their own quarters. After some period in rented, small housing, they purchase a modest home, and in ensuing years they improve this home and perhaps move into larger quarters. By the time they retire, their own children have left home, and the large suburban house gives way to a smaller residence (and a tax-free capital gain). Similarly sized cohorts move through this process in orderly form, and increases or decreases in the housing stock are orderly and predictable. Now consider what happens when young adults live alone once they finish school. Demand for small residences—apartments, in large part, but increasingly homes—increases while demand for larger homes, which still appeal primarily to couples planning children, remains stable. However, since children leave home earlier, the average tenure in the larger home decreases, and eventually supply exceeds demand. Now say that young adults and retiring adults simultaneously move to another region. The demand for smaller quarters drops back toward its uncomplicated level in the source region, but it increases sharply in the receiving region. There is little immediate demand for larger houses in the receiving region, but as the immigrant young adults begin bearing children, this changes, and demand for larger homes rises. Since builders are busy with smaller residences (condominiums, for example), the prices of larger homes rise sharply. Builders shift their efforts accordingly. However, since the new parents are planning to have fewer children than earlier parents did, they respond to increased house prices by improving their small quarters instead of buying new houses. Builders respond accordingly. And so on; the housing business oscillates widely.

The major change in household structures we project for the New England, Mid-Atlantic, and East North Central regions is increased single headship. This trend is orderly, even given high emigration, and the major dislocation it causes is competition between poor families and affluent single adults for the same small living quarters. This is the basis for much of the tumult surrounding urban condominium conversions. The late fertility common among northern women delays the movement of single adults into large, child-oriented homes, but this probably is a temporary lag. In any case, the major effect is to depress the demand for large houses, reducing the incentive for older occupants to sell and enter the more heated market for smaller residences. The market is stable, particularly if cohort size is declining and balancing increased headship.

The change we project for the South Central and Mountain regions is more dramatic. Demand for small housing should rise sharply as young adults move into the regions, and demand should gradually rise for larger houses as well. In some states young migrants will compete with older migrants for small residences. As young adults have children and move into larger houses, they will vacate smaller residences. In many places there will be a depressed market for these until the baby boomlet—the children of the young migrants—is ready to occupy individual homes. (Recall that we project retiree migration to distribute itself differently in the future, meaning flows to these regions—and the consequent demand for small residences—will slow somewhat.) This boomlet will be sharper in South Central than in Mountain. Thus changes in headship patterns and housing demand will be somewhat cyclic, with correspondingly unstable effects on housing markets. The Pacific region combines substantial immigration of young adults with substantial rates of divorce and separation, and therefore its housing demand should be similar. Here, however, housing prices are extremely high, and the effects of this on demand (and migration itself) are hard to project.

Unlike the West South Central, Mountain, and Pacific regions, the South Atlantic region had a well-developed infrastructure before it began to attract migrants. This worked to the advantage of retirees, who chose to live in warm, established communities that provided suitable housing and services as an inducement. The effects of this migration were orderly and predictable. Young adults were another matter. They could not be concentrated in retirement-oriented communities, since the jobs they came to take were elsewhere. The well-developed infrastructure made it difficult to expand housing where young adults came to work. The supply of larger homes was even more constrained, and thus it was difficult for young adults to raise families without sacrificing comfort. The sharply reduced fertility in the South Atlantic may be one result of this, and it is among the factors that lead us to predict decelerating growth in the region.

Working Conditions

As the baby-boom cohorts entered the labor market, there were large numbers of applicants for most jobs, and as a result, companies could afford to ignore human-resource development. As the smaller cohorts born in the late 1960s replace the baby-boom cohorts, a process we graphed in Figure 3.6, this will change. Companies will have to compete for entry-level workers, and the resources they devote to this competition will necessarily reduce those available to reward continuing employees. But continuing employees will demand rewards. Their numbers will make the typical nonpecuniary reward, promotion, possible for a decreasing percentage of the cohorts, and with neither money nor promotion, employees' dissatisfaction will increase.

This is a national problem, a result of the second bulge in fertility we described above. It will affect all regions but will hit hardest those that, like New England, can expect steady declines in young-adult population. The southern regions will get temporary relief when the baby-boom cohorts' children—the third bulge—enter the labor force and enable employers to select rather than recruit once more, but this will be short-lived. The Mountain and Pacific regions, on the other hand, should experience a relatively small decline in the size of later cohorts, a result of above-average fertility across the childbearing ages. The resulting steady supply of entry-level workers competing for jobs will enable businesses to balance their resources between attracting new employees and rewarding long-term ones.

A similar analysis applies to pensions, which for the most part guarantee a certain pension level in return for a certain rate of contribution. When pensioner cohorts are smaller than worker cohorts, small contribution rates can fund large pensions. When pensioner cohorts are larger than worker cohorts, it takes large contributions to fund even modest pensions. The conflict between workers and pensioners comes later than the conflict between new hires and long-term employees, but it results from the same age imbalance.

Urban Life

As headship increases among single adults, the size of the average household declines. This has several effects. First, the density of population in existing areas—cities, for the most part—decreases. Second, the per-capita cost of maintaining these areas increases, since many costs do not decline with population. Third, the city's needs for retail trade and services change. Decreased population density generally means improved living conditions, as traffic, queues, and so on decline; we discussed this in Chapter 3. Thus, although Boston has lost population over the past years, many residents assert that the quality of life in the city has improved. This improved quality of life comes at a price, since the cost of maintaining a street (or any urban system) is about the same, whether it is crowded or not. And the entire change is accompanied by considerable economic dislocation, as once important activities, such as schooling, become less important and others, such as restaurants and redevelopment programs, become more so.

This scenario holds only if the number of households remains constant or grows slowly. In a growing city, the quality of life can drop as proliferating households jam fixed urban systems, leading to traffic, pollution, water shortages, and so on. For a time, per-capita costs also drop, since existing urban systems serve increased numbers. But eventually capital investment is required—for waterworks and sewerage, perhaps, or new roads—and in these times the price is very high. Since growing cities are often quite diverse, all sorts of services and trade must grow, and as they compete for employees and commercial space, costs can rise. Denver exhibits many of these symptoms.

It is tempting to say that Denver represents cities in fast-growth regions and that Boston represents cities in no-growth regions, but doing so neglects the nonmetropolitan element in regional growth and the substantial variation among cities. Thus general predictions are difficult.

Social Services

Children need schools. Working adults need rapid transit, roads, and inexpensive housing. Families need parks, playgrounds, and zoos. The elderly need senior-citizen centers, homemaker services, and convenient housing. When an area has a lot of children, it builds schools. When the children age, it closes the schools and upgrades rapid transit and expressway systems, and so on down the list. When different age groups are simultaneously large, higher taxes and competition for scarce funds result. Older regions often have all the required institutions, and changes in the age structure merely cause reallocations of operating expenses. Less mature regions often must create services when they become necessary, and either the cost is high or—if it is too high—the need goes unmet.

We described in Chapter 3 the changes in age structure different regions can expect, and we extended that discussion above. Clearly the less mature fast-growth regions—South Central and Mountain—can expect conflict over social services. The resolution may be to require individuals to purchase social services privately, or it may be to make the required public investment; in either case, costs of living will increase to reflect the necessary investment. Alternatively, individuals requiring certain services may move to areas that provide them. This used to be common for suburban parents of young children, and it is not atypical for working adults to move away from cities or towns that emphasize social services for children or the elderly.

Politics

Here we are on slippery ground; many a prediction has slipped and fallen on a political projection. The dimensions of political change are clear from the preceding outline: There will be contention around the allocation of inexpensive housing (to poor adults or affluent young singles), around work rewards (for new, long-term, or retired employees), and around social spending (for schools, housing, or hospitals). The nation's age structure exacerbates all this, since the baby-boom cohorts will gradually settle into family life in substantial homes and act to conserve what they have amassed just when the early bulge overloads hospitals and the third bulge needs schools. These political conflicts will vary from region to region as the other impacts do.

More serious, however, is political conflict among regions, which has always been important in the United States but which seems to have moved away from accommodation and toward confrontation in recent years. So long as total growth was substantial, regional differences merely entailed different shares of new activity. As total growth slows, regional differences begin to mean that one region gains only when another loses, a much more difficult situation politically. Lester Thurow has pursued this observation in *The Zero–Sum Society:**

Our political and economic structure simply isn't able to cope with an economy that has a substantial zero-sum element. . . .

The problem with zero-sum games is that the essence of problem solving is loss allocation. But this is precisely what our political process is least capable of doing. When there are economic gains to be allocated, our political process can allocate them. Where there are large economic losses to be allocated, our political process is paralyzed. And with political paralysis comes economic paralysis. . . .

Consider the interstate highway system. . . . [M]ost observers would agree that the interstate highway system could not have been built if it had been proposed in the mid-1970s rather than in the mid-1950s.

Exactly the same factors that would prevent the initiation of an interstate highway system would also prevent the initiation of any alternative transportation system. A few years ago, when a high-speed rail system was being considered for the Boston-Washington corridor, a former governor of Connecticut announced that he would veto any relocation of the Boston-to-New York line on the grounds that it would be of prime benefit to those at either end of the line, but would tear up Connecticut homes. . . .

The Balkanization of nations is a worldwide phenomenon that the United States has not escaped. Regions and localities are less and less willing to incur costs that will primarily help people in other parts of the same country. Consider the development of the coalfields of Wyoming and Montana. There is no question that most of the benefits will accrue to those living in urban areas in the rest of the country while most of the costs will be imposed on those living in that region. As a result, the local population objects. More coal mining might be good for the United States, but it will be bad

---

*From *The Zero-Sum Society*, by Lester Thurow. Copyright © 1980 by Basic Books, Inc. By permission of Basic Books, Inc., Publishers, New York.

*for local constituents. Therefore they will impose as many delays
and uncertainties as possible. (pp. 11–14)*

Thurow argues that avoiding interregional strife is possible, but
only if regions act on the basis of their communal interests rather
than their parochial ones.

This is the appropriate point to return to the question we raised
a few pages back: Are regional differences or national trends more
important? There is little question that growth in the United States
has slowed, and that it will remain modest. For a nation accustomed to making relatively easy choices—namely, how to allocate
increased benefits—this requires a major and difficult change to
choices involving trade-offs and cutbacks. No region will act as
though it is a zero-sum society until it is forced to do so, but no
region will be able to avoid difficult trade-offs. This means that
there are lessons for currently prosperous regions in the experi-
ences and actions of their stable or declining counterparts. Janet
Pack, in a similar but earlier analysis of regional trends, concluded
that renewed national growth was the only hope for the slow-
growing regions. It is probably true that renewed growth would
reduce regional disparities, but renewed growth is unlikely. We,
in contrast, see in the near-term responses of these slow-growth
regions the first opportunity to arrive at social, economic, and
political conventions suited to the nation's stable future. Progress
toward these is essential not only for currently depressed regions
but also, in the longer term, for the others. Thus the answer to
our question: National trends are more important than regional
ones. But regional trends give us invaluable information about
future changes in the nation. By investigating them, we can identify and act on the national policy issues of the 1980s.

Appendix A

OFFICIAL PROJECTIONS

There are two basic ways to project regional growth: by modeling regional economies directly, treating each as a separate entity; or by disaggregating national projections, treating regions as similarly structured, interdependent units among which national product, population, income, and so forth are parceled. The former method, though appealing in principle, requires considerably more data than are usually available. Moreover, to be credible such "bottom-up" projections must imply reasonable national totals and therefore must take national projections into account. For these reasons virtually all regional projections are to some extent "top-down," in that they project regional shares of national totals. The specific methodologies underlying different regional projection series vary enormously, but nevertheless the fundamental approach—dividing national growth among regions—is the same.

In this appendix we focus on the substance of different official projection series. A given projection series implies a set of growth rates for different regions (or more often, different states or economic areas, which we have combined into the nine Census regions). The regions' growth rates can be compared, and the comparisons yield regional rankings. Given several projection series, one can make another comparison, between the sets of regional growth rates the different projections yield. The entire exercise can then be repeated for different regional attributes. Methodological differences account for some interseries differences, but this effect probably is moderate. Assumptions about future trends account for other differences. The several projection series we review start from different assumptions, primarily because they were done in different years and therefore drew on different historical periods for "recent" data. National growth slowed sharply

135

around 1970, in part because there was a recession in the business cycle and in part because (it now appears) long-term trends changed. Projectors who allocated a substantial part of the overall slowdown to the recession, typically those who worked before 1974, projected renewed growth in older industrial regions. As we will see, projectors who allocated the slowdown to long-term trends saw things differently.

In Chapter 2 we devoted more attention to the economic links among the three regional attributes we discuss here: earnings, employment, and population. For now we will focus on the growth rates of these variables through 1990, commenting on the two sorts of variation—between regions and between projection series—mentioned above. Appendix C contains tables giving absolute levels, national shares, and growth rates for each attribute through the year 1990.

Virtually all regional projections come from six sources, three government and three private. The three government sources are the Census Bureau, the Bureau of Economic Analysis, and the Oak Ridge National Laboratory. The first two are agencies of the U. S. Commerce Department, and the last is funded by the Energy Department. The three private sources are the National Planning Association, Chase Econometrics, and Data Resources, Inc. We analyze only the "official" series, which (with the National Planning Association series) are also the only ones whose methodology is open to scrutiny.

The Census Bureau projects population according to different assumptions about fertility and migration. We consider here only the projections of Series II-A (which assumes completed fertility of 2.1 children per woman and 1965–1975 migration patterns) and Series II-B (which assumes the same fertility and 1970–1975 migration patterns). A more detailed discussion of Census methodology appears in Chapter 3 and underlies our somewhat different population projections in Chapter 2.

The Bureau of Economic Analysis projects earnings, employment, population, and personal income. In theory it does so every five years, but in fact there have been four series, issued in 1972, 1974, 1977, and 1980 publications. The 1972 series relied on several unrealistic assumptions, and we agree with the professional consensus that it should be ignored. The 1974 series corresponds roughly to the Census II-A assumptions, though its methodology for translating national totals into regional shares is very different (more on this later). The 1977 "interim" series revised the 1974 series to reflect the national slowdown that began around 1970, but it projected only earnings and population. The 1980 series (which, on a five-year schedule, should have been issued in 1979) reflects more recent historical trends and a somewhat modified methodology.

The Oak Ridge National Laboratory's Multiregion model projects population and employment. Its projections are considerably more detailed than any but the BEA 1980 series, but for the present we examine only the aggregate state figures. An MR-1 version is based on model equations that fit the 1960–1970 period accurately; an MR-2 version is adjusted to fit the 1970–1975 period more accurately. (In each case the time period has pervasive effects on the model's equations, instead of simply determining migration rates as it does in the Census methodology.)

Earnings

Figure A.1 portrays earnings growth rates projected for approximately the 1970–1990 period. All figures are in 1972 dollars; we have converted the BEA 74 and 77 projections, which were in 1967 dollars, to 1972 dollars. (We used the personal-consumption-expenditures implicit-price deflator, 1.230 on a 1967 base of 1.00.) The base year for growth is 1969 because 1970 was a recession year, particularly for some regions (and even more so for some states). The earnings observations for 1970 are a bit below the long-term growth paths for the regions, which would overstate growth rates somewhat. In focusing on the more normal 1969 year as an interim base period, we follow the example of BEA, which used 1969 as a base year in its recent 1980 projections.

We do have a minor statistical problem for 1969, however. There are two different earnings series available for 1969. The first, denoted 1969-I in Table A.1, is the series that was available at the time BEA made its 1974 and 1977 projections. The second, denoted 1969-II, is the revised series that underlies the BEA 80 projections. The differences are not totally trivial, especially for some states. Since differences might introduce irrelevant variations into growth rates, we adopt the following procedure. In Appendix B we present both series for reference. We use 1969-I as the base for growth rates implied by the BEA 74 and 77

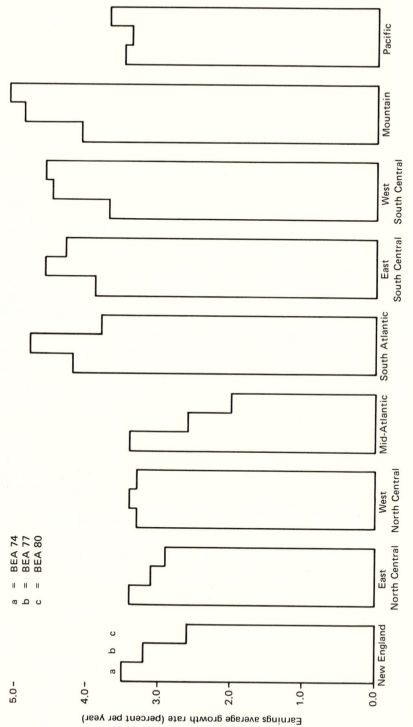

Figure A.1   Projections of Earnings Growth Rates, 1970–1990.

Table A.1 Earnings (billions of 1972 dollars)

Census Region	Historical					1990 Projection			2000 Projection		
	1960 (1)	1969-I (2)	1969-II (3)	1970 (4)	1978 (5)	BEA 74 (6)	BEA 77 (7)	BEA 80 (8)	BEA 74 (9)	BEA 77 (10)	BEA 80 (11)
New England	27.9	41.8	41.3	42.3	47.8	86.7	80.5	71.0	122.5	107.2	90.6
Mid-Atlantic	99.2	140.8	138.4	142.2	150.6	283.1	239.4	211.6	394.9	297.0	258.0
East North Central	98.9	148.9	146.1	147.0	179.2	299.7	284.7	271.3	416.4	365.5	347.0
West North Central	35.1	51.7	50.9	52.6	67.1	102.5	103.3	102.4	141.1	135.5	134.1
South Atlantic	54.4	94.4	93.1	97.6	128.9	221.9	253.7	206.8	321.9	374.9	281.2
East South Central	20.4	32.9	32.3	33.4	46.2	74.0	85.3	78.8	105.9	122.7	108.9
West South Central	34.2	54.8	53.7	56.4	83.3	116.9	137.6	142.0	165.6	200.4	198.5
Mountain	16.2	24.9	24.5	26.2	40.1	57.5	68.2	71.5	81.9	99.8	102.2
Pacific	62.3	100.1	99.1	99.9	135.9	205.0	201.9	215.7	288.3	269.7	289.7
U.S. Total	448.5	690.2	679.5	697.5	879.2	1447.4	1454.7	1371.1	2038.5	1972.8	1810.1

SOURCE: Cols. 1, 2, 4, 7, 10, BEA 77 projections; cols. 3, 5, 8, 11, BEA 80 projections; cols. 6, 9, BEA 74 projections.

series, but we use 1969-II for the growth rates implied in the
BEA 80.

According to the BEA 74 columns in Figure A-1, New England
has a stable position relative to the nation: Its growth rate between
1969 and 1990 is just below the national rate. The Pacific region
is similar. There are relative declines in the Mid-Atlantic, East
North Central, and West North Central regions, but these declines
are not very strong. There are relatively large increases in the
South Atlantic and Mountain regions and a more modest increase
in the two South Central regions.

Now, however, note the substantial revisions for 1990 in BEA
77 by comparing its columns to the BEA 74 columns in Figure
A.1. There is general acceleration of the trends projected three
years earlier. Now New England and East North Central decline
sharply, joining Mid-Atlantic, whose decline is even more evident
than it was in the 1974 series. The relative advantages of the four
Southern and Mountain regions are increased. The West North
Central and Pacific regions are not revised much at all. This sort
of review is somewhat tedious, but we shall see in later figures
the same basic pattern in the revised projections. By describing
it here at the beginning, we can move through the remaining
variables more quickly.

The BEA 80 column shows the revisions for 1990 in this series.
Several revisions extend the interim ones. The Mid-Atlantic and
New England regions are revised substantially downward again,
since the projectors had seen the longer decline through the 1970s
in these regions. The West South Central and Mountain regions
are revised slightly upward again. However, the BEA 80 projections do not uniformly extend the BEA 77 revisions. The Pacific
is revised up a bit. East South Central is actually revised back
down toward the BEA 74 projection. The East North Central, on
the other hand, is not revised this time. The West North Central
region is not revised much. The really striking feature of BEA 80,
however, is that the South Atlantic is now sharply reduced, more
than reversing the upward revision of BEA 77. The explanation
of BEA 77 is skimpy, so we do not know why there was such a
"blip" in the time track of projection exercises. Since BEA 80
erased this blip, we conclude BEA 77 had some features that were
later found to be objectionable.

It is useful to compare the BEA 80 projections of growth rates
with the 1969–1978 historical growth rates, thus comparing the

most recent projection of the future with the most recent past (data for this comparison are in Table A.2). The declining trend in New England, East North Central, and Mid-Atlantic reflects historical trends, but in all these cases the growth rates are projected to be much closer to the nation's than they actually were in 1969–1978. BEA 80 thus clearly projects a marked reduction in the relative depression of growth that characterized these industrialized regions in the 1970s. The West North Central region remains close to the nation, as it has been. The South Atlantic region's relative growth advantage is much smaller than its historical counterpart, rather surprising for a region largely in the sunbelt. We discussed this in Chapter 2. The Pacific's growth is also projected to be slower than its historical growth. The East South Central, West South Central, and Mountain regions are expected to grow much more rapidly than the nation in the rest of the century, but their advantage is much less than it was in 1969–1978.

The interregional variation in growth rates is projected to be much less in the 1980s than it was in the 1970s. The growth advantages of the South and West are much smaller, as are the disadvantages of the Northeast and Midwest. The national growth rate is projected to rise substantially in the 1980s, and that rise will have an especially favorable effect on the industrial regions.

Employment

We now turn to projections of employment growth, which results from interaction between demand and supply in the labor market. Figure A.2 gives the relevant growth rates in a format similar to that of Figure A.1, excluding BEA 77 (which did not project employment) and adding the two Multiregion projections (MR-1 and MR-2).

We again have a problem with the base year. In its documentation for BEA 74, BEA presented employment data for 1970, in spite of the fact that it had used 1969 as a base for earnings projections. BEA 74 used 1970 as a base for employment because the employment data necessary for projections were then available only for Census years, thus for 1970 but not 1969. However, in its most recent projections, BEA used employment data for the 1969 base year, on a basis consistent with the projected values.

Table A.2 Back-Up Table for Figure A.1: Earnings, Average Annual Rates of Growth (percent per year)

Census Region	1969–1978 (1)	1969–1990			1990–2000			1978–1990
		BEA 74 (2)	BEA 77 (3)	BEA 80 (4)	BEA 74 (5)	BEA 77 (6)	BEA 80 (7)	BEA 80 (8)
New England	1.6	3.5	3.2	2.6	3.5	2.9	2.5	3.4
Mid-Atlantic	.9	3.4	2.6	2.0	3.3	2.2	2.0	2.9
East North Central	2.3	3.4	3.1	2.9	3.3	2.5	2.5	3.5
West North Central	3.1	3.3	3.4	3.3	3.2	2.8	2.7	3.6
South Atlantic	3.7	4.2	4.8	3.8	3.8	4.0	3.1	4.0
East South Central	4.1	3.9	4.6	4.3	3.6	3.7	3.3	4.6
West South Central	5.0	3.7	4.5	4.6	3.5	3.8	3.4	4.5
Mountain	5.6	4.1	4.9	5.1	3.6	3.9	3.6	4.9
Pacific	3.6	3.5	3.4	3.7	3.5	2.9	3.0	3.9
U.S. Total	2.9	3.6	3.6	3.3	3.5	3.1	2.8	3.8

SOURCE: Terminal years from correspondingly labeled columns in Table A.1.
Base years: 1969-I from Table A.1 for cols. 2, 3, 5, 6; 1969-II from Table A.1 for cols. 1, 4, 7; 1978 from Table A.1.

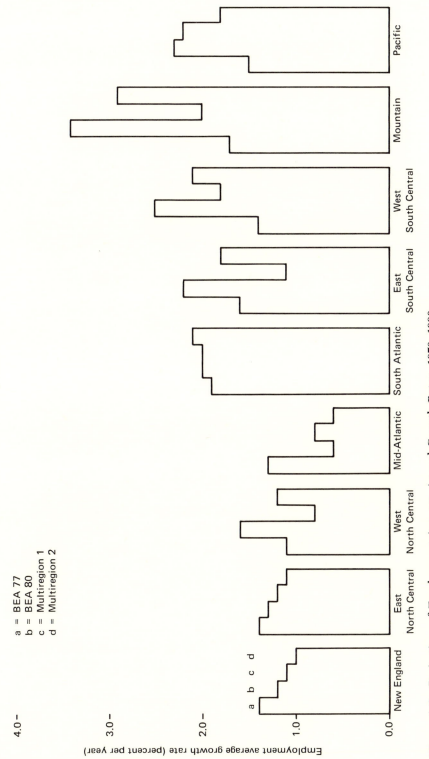

Figure A.2 Projections of Employment Average Annual Growth Rates, 1970–1990.

The 1969 data are apparently on a somewhat different conceptual basis from the 1970 data: The difference in the national total is over 6 million employees, or 7.5 percent, far too big a discrepancy to be accounted for by one year's passage of time (especially as 1970 was a low-growth year). To resolve the problem, we have computed growth rates for the BEA 74 and Multiregion projections using 1970 as the base, but growth rates for BEA 80 using 1969 as the base. We have thus computed the growth rates using conceptually consistent data for the base and terminal years.

In BEA 74 regional variation in employment growth rates is small. Only the relative advantage of the South Atlantic and the relative disadvantage of the West North Central region are substantial. These features are similar to those of earnings growth in Figure A.1.

As we would expect, the interregional variation is greater for MR-2 (which reflects the divergent trends of the early 1970s) than for MR-1 (which reflects trends through 1970). The deviations of MR-2 from MR-1 are as expected. The effects of the more recent migration patterns used in MR-2 are to project that the Mid-Atlantic and Pacific regions will grow less rapidly than projected in MR-1, and that the West North Central, both South Central, and the Mountain regions will grow more rapidly. The difference between MR-1 and MR-2 is very large for East South Central and Mountain because migration patterns changed sharply between 1970 and 1975 in those regions.

The Multiregion projections show much more interregional variation than does BEA 74. The Multiregion exercise was completed well after BEA 74 but also a few years before BEA 80. Both Multiregion series differ from BEA 74. Growth in the New England, Mid-Atlantic, and East North Central regions is smaller in Multiregion, whereas growth in the West South Central, Mountain, and Pacific regions is larger. The mixed case of West North Central is not surprising. MR-1 shows a decline from BEA 74 because the migration patterns of the 1960s were unfavorable to West North Central, but in light of the more favorable patterns of the 1970s, MR-2 shows a very slight increase over BEA 74. However, the Multiregion projections are puzzling for the East South Central and South Atlantic regions. MR-1 and MR-2 project the South Atlantic at almost identical rates, nearly the same high rate as BEA 74. In the East South Central, MR-1 shows a decided decline from BEA 74, but MR-2 shows a slight increase. BEA 80 projects much more growth than MR-2 in all regions but particularly in the West North Central, East South Central, West South Central, Mountain, and Pacific regions—even more optimistic than MR-2.

As for the projections, BEA 74 projected relatively little change in relative earnings between 1970 and 1990; a continued catching up for the East South Central is the only major movement. Although we have 9 years to go until 1990, it appears BEA 74 erred by missing the relative decline in New England and the stability in East North Central, by being a bit overoptimistic in West North Central and Mountain, and by restraining its optimism in West South Central. BEA 80 revised BEA 74 somewhat but mostly to recognize the relative growth already apparent in 1978: It projects very little additional change between 1978 and 1990 except in East South Central.

Population

The great regional disparities in the recent history of population growth, about which we said more in Chapter 3, are evident in Figure A.3. As before, we use 1969 as the base year for BEA projections and 1970 for the Census Bureau and Multiregion projections. Population growth rates vary more than the earnings and employment growth rates reviewed above. The extreme observations for the Mid-Atlantic (low) and the Mountain (high) regions add to the variation.

As we look across Figure A.3, we see the revisions, familiar by now, of the BEA 74 numbers. A similar pattern is also evident if we look at the later Census Bureau and Multiregion projections. Even the Census A series, which assumes 1965–1975 migration trends, shows the more recent pattern of slower growth in the New England, Mid-Atlantic, and East North Central regions and faster growth in the West South Central and Mountain regions. Census B, which reflects 1970–1975 migration patterns, is very close to BEA 80, except that it projects much higher growth for South Atlantic. But remember that in BEA 80 the South Atlantic region's economic growth rates were revised sharply downward, as were BEA 80 population growth rates. The 1980 revisions leave BEA's projections of the South Atlantic growth rate through 1990 lower than Census A, Census B, or either Multiregion series.

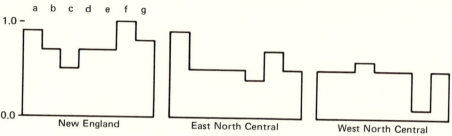

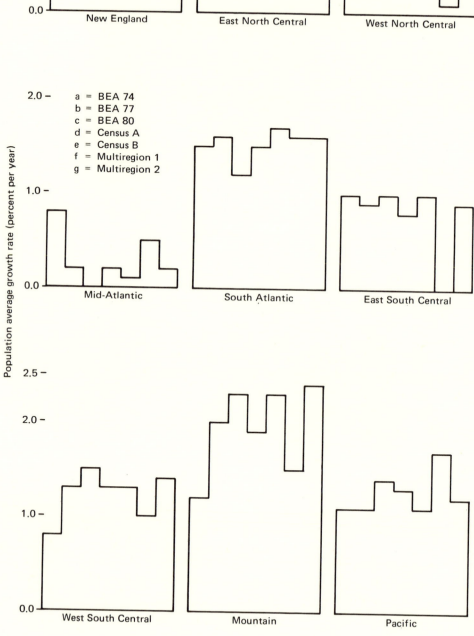

a = BEA 74
b = BEA 77
c = BEA 80
d = Census A
e = Census B
f = Multiregion 1
g = Multiregion 2

Population average growth rate (percent per year)

Census B is actually quite close to the BEA 77 projection for South Atlantic.

The two Multiregion projections again diverge from each other for a number of regions—considerably more so than the Census projections differ from each other, although within-source differences are due in each case to different migration assumptions. The most notable examples of divergence between MR-1 and MR-2 are in East South Central and Mountain. Divergence is also sizable for West North Central, West South Central, and Pacific. MR-2 is predictable, giving generally lower growth rates than MR-1 for the New England, Mid-Atlantic, East North Central, and Pacific regions and generally higher ones for the West North Central, West South Central, and Mountain regions. The MR-1 projection is really quite anomalous in predicting essentially no population growth for the East South Central region under older migration assumptions. The turnaround in the migration patterns in the 1970s in the East South Central and the West North Central apparently receives more weight in the Multiregion econometric model than in any of the other projection methodologies. MR-2, BEA 80, and Census B are all quite similar; the main difference is that Census B and MR-2 project a significantly higher rate of growth for the South Atlantic than BEA 80 does.

Figure A.3 Projections of Population Average Annual Growth Rates 1970–1990.

Table A.3 Earnings, Percentage of U.S. Total

Census Region	Historical				1990 Projection			2000 Projection		
	1960	1969-I	1969-II	1978	BEA 74	BEA 77	BEA 80	BEA 74	BEA 77	BEA 80
New England	6.2	6.0	6.1	5.4	6.0	5.5	5.2	6.0	5.4	5.0
Mid-Atlantic	22.1	20.4	20.4	17.1	19.6	16.5	15.4	19.4	15.1	14.3
East North Central	22.1	21.6	21.5	20.4	20.7	19.6	19.8	20.4	18.5	19.2
West North Central	7.8	7.5	7.5	7.6	7.1	7.1	7.5	6.9	6.9	7.4
South Atlantic	12.1	13.7	13.7	14.7	15.3	17.4	15.1	15.8	19.0	15.5
East South Central	4.5	4.8	4.8	5.3	5.1	5.9	5.8	5.2	6.2	6.0
West South Central	7.6	7.9	7.9	9.5	8.1	9.5	10.4	8.1	10.2	11.0
Mountain	3.6	3.6	3.6	4.6	4.0	4.7	5.2	4.0	5.1	5.6
Pacific	13.9	14.5	14.6	15.5	14.2	13.9	15.7	14.1	13.7	16.0
U.S. Total	100.0	100.0	100.0	100.0	100.0	100.0	100.0	100.0	100.0	100.0

SOURCE: Table A.1 (unrounded data).

Table A.4 Employment (in millions)

Census Region	Historical				1990 Projection				2000 Projection	
	1960 (1)	1969 (2)	1970 (3)	1978 (4)	BEA 74 (5)	BEA 80 (6)	MR-1 (7)	MR-2 (8)	BEA 74 (9)	BEA 80 (10)
New England	4.1	5.2	4.9	5.8	6.4	6.7	6.1	5.9	7.2	7.0
Mid-Atlantic	13.2	15.9	14.7	16.2	19.2	17.9	17.6	16.7	21.3	17.8
East North Central	13.4	17.0	15.7	18.9	21.0	22.1	20.1	19.4	23.0	23.0
West North Central	5.7	7.0	6.4	8.3	7.9	9.7	7.5	8.0	8.5	10.3
South Atlantic	9.5	13.1	12.2	16.2	17.6	20.0	18.2	18.5	19.9	21.9
East South Central	4.0	4.9	4.6	6.1	6.4	7.7	5.8	6.6	7.0	8.5
West South Central	5.9	7.7	7.2	10.1	9.4	13.0	10.3	10.8	10.4	14.6
Mountain	2.4	3.3	3.1	4.9	4.4	6.7	4.7	5.5	4.9	7.7
Pacific	8.1	11.3	10.6	14.4	14.1	18.2	16.1	15.0	15.7	20.1
U.S. Total	66.4	85.4	79.3	101.1	106.4	122.0	106.5	106.5	117.9	130.9

SOURCE: Cols. 1, 3, 5, 9, BEA 74 projections; cols. 2, 4, 6, 10, BEA 80 projections; cols. 7, 11 Multiregion MR-1 projections; cols. 8, 12, Multiregion MR-2 projections.

Table A.5   Back-Up Table for Figure A.2: Employment, Average Annual Rates of Growth (percent per year)

Census Region	1969–1978 Actual (1)	1970–1990 BEA 74 (2)	1970–1990 BEA 77 (3)	1969–1990 BEA 80 (4)	1970–1990 MR-1 (5)	1970–1990 MR-2 (6)	1990–2000 BEA 74 (7)	1990–2000 BEA 80 (8)	1978–1990 BEA 80 (11)
New England	1.2	1.4	N	1.2	1.1	1.0	1.0	.4	1.2
Mid-Atlantic	.2	1.3	O	.6	.8	.6	1.0	0.0	.8
East North Central	1.2	1.4	T	1.3	1.2	1.1	.9	.4	1.3
West North Central	1.9	1.1	A	1.6	.8	1.2	.8	.6	1.3
South Atlantic	2.4	1.9	V	2.0	2.0	2.1	1.2	.9	1.7
East South Central	2.4	1.6	A I	2.2	1.1	1.8	1.0	1.0	2.0
West South Central	3.1	1.4	L	2.5	1.8	2.1	1.0	1.2	2.1
Mountain	4.5	1.7	A B	3.4	2.0	2.9	1.1	1.4	2.6
Pacific	2.8	1.5	L	2.3	2.2	1.8	1.1	1.0	1.9
U.S. Total	1.9	1.5	E	1.7	1.5	1.5	1.0	.7	1.6

SOURCE: Both base and terminal years are from similarly labeled columns in Table A.4.

Table A.6 Employment, Percentage of U.S. Total

Census Region	Historical				1990 Projection				2000 Projection	
	1960 (1)	1969 (2)	1970 (3)	1978 (4)	BEA 74 (5)	BEA 80 (6)	MR-1 (7)	MR-2 (8)	BEA 74 (9)	BEA 80 (10)
New England	6.2	6.1	6.2	5.8	6.1	5.5	5.7	5.6	6.1	5.3
Mid-Atlantic	19.9	18.6	18.6	16.1	18.1	14.6	16.5	15.6	18.0	13.6
East North Central	20.2	19.8	19.8	18.7	19.7	18.1	18.9	18.3	19.5	17.6
West North Central	8.6	8.2	8.1	8.2	7.4	8.0	7.1	7.6	7.2	7.8
South Atlantic	14.3	15.3	15.3	16.1	16.5	16.4	17.1	17.1	16.8	16.7
East South Central	6.0	5.8	5.8	6.0	6.0	6.3	5.4	6.2	6.0	6.5
West South Central	8.9	9.0	9.1	10.0	8.9	10.7	9.7	10.2	8.8	11.2
Mountain	3.7	3.9	3.9	4.9	4.1	5.5	4.4	5.2	4.1	5.9
Pacific	12.2	13.2	13.2	14.3	13.3	14.9	15.2	14.1	13.3	15.3
U.S. Total	100.0	100.0	100.0	100.0	100.0	100.0	100.0	100.0	100.0	100.0

SOURCE: Similarly labeled columns of Table A.4 (unrounded data).

Table A.7 Population, Historical Data (in millions)

Census Region	1960	1969	1970	1978
New England	10.5	11.7	11.8	12.3
Mid-Atlantic	34.2	36.9	37.2	36.8
East North Central	36.2	39.9	40.3	41.2
West North Central	15.4	16.2	16.3	17.0
South Atlantic	26.0	30.3	30.7	34.6
East South Central	12.1	12.8	12.8	14.0
West South Central	17.0	19.1	19.3	22.0
Mountain	6.9	8.2	8.3	10.3
Pacific	21.2	26.2	26.5	29.8
U.S. Total	179.3	201.3	203.3	218.1

SOURCE: 1960 and 1970, Census Bureau (decennial census); 1969 and 1978, BEA 80 (midyear estimates).

Table A.8 Population Projected for 1990

Census Region	BEA			Census		Multiregion	
	1974	1977	1980	II-A	II-B	MR-1	MR-2
New England	14.1	13.7	13.1	13.7	13.6	14.6	13.8
Mid-Atlantic	43.2	38.9	36.9	39.1	38.2	41.0	38.6
East North Central	47.7	44.3	44.1	44.8	43.3	46.2	44.3
West North Central	18.0	17.8	18.4	18.0	18.1	16.5	18.1
South Atlantic	41.2	42.2	40.1	41.2	42.8	41.8	42.5
East South Central	15.7	15.3	15.8	15.1	15.5	12.7	15.4
West South Central	22.8	25.3	26.1	24.8	25.3	23.6	25.4
Mountain	10.5	12.4	13.1	12.1	12.9	11.2	13.3
Pacific	32.7	33.0	35.3	34.2	33.4	37.5	33.6
U.S. Total	246.0	243.0	243.0	243.0	243.0	245.1	245.1

SOURCE: Projection series identified by heading.

Table A.9 Back-Up Table for Figure A.3: Population, Average Annual Rates of Growth (percent per year)

Census Region	1969–1978 (1)	1969–1990		BEA 80 (4)	1978–1990 BEA 80 (5)	1970–1990			
		BEA 74 (2)	BEA 77 (3)			Census A (6)	Census B (7)	MR-1 (8)	MR-2 (9)
New England	0.5	0.9	0.7	0.5	0.6	0.7	0.7	1.0	0.8
Mid-Atlantic	0.0	0.8	0.2	0.0	0.0	0.2	0.1	0.5	0.2
East North Central	0.4	0.9	0.5	0.5	0.6	0.5	0.4	0.7	0.5
West North Central	0.5	0.5	0.5	0.6	0.7	0.5	0.5	0.1	0.5
South Atlantic	1.5	1.5	1.6	1.2	1.2	1.5	1.7	1.6	1.6
East South Central	1.0	1.0	0.9	1.0	1.0	.8	1.0	0.0	0.9
West South Central	1.6	0.8	1.3	1.5	1.4	1.3	1.3	1.0	1.4
Mountain	2.6	1.2	2.0	2.3	2.1	1.9	2.3	1.5	2.4
Pacific	1.5	1.1	1.1	1.4	1.4	1.3	1.1	1.7	1.2
U.S. Total	0.9	1.0	0.9	0.9	0.9	0.9	0.9	0.9	0.9

SOURCE: Cols. 1, 4, 5, BEA 80; cols. 2–3, 1969 from BEA 80, 1990 from projection series identified in heading; cols. 6–9, 1970 from Bureau of Census (decennial census), 1990 from projection series identified in heading.

Table A.10 Population, Percentage of U.S. Total (Historical)

Census Region	1960	1969	1970	1978
New England	5.9	5.8	5.8	5.6
Mid-Atlantic	19.1	18.4	18.3	16.9
East North Central	20.2	19.8	19.8	18.9
West North Central	8.6	8.0	8.0	7.8
South Atlantic	14.5	15.1	15.1	15.9
East South Central	6.7	6.3	6.3	6.4
West South Central	9.5	9.5	9.5	10.1
Mountain	3.8	4.1	4.1	4.7
Pacific	11.8	13.0	13.1	13.7
U.S. Total	100.0	100.0	100.0	100.0

SOURCE: Table A.7 (unrounded data).

Table A.11 Population, Percentage of U.S. Total, 1990

Census Region	BEA			Census		Multiregion	
	1974	1977	1980	A	B	MR-1	MR-2
New England	5.7	5.6	5.4	5.6	5.6	5.9	5.6
Mid-Atlantic	17.6	16.0	15.2	16.1	15.7	16.7	15.7
East North Central	19.4	18.2	18.1	18.5	17.8	18.9	18.1
West North Central	7.3	7.3	7.6	7.4	7.4	6.7	7.4
South Atlantic	16.7	17.4	16.5	16.9	17.6	17.1	17.3
East South Central	6.4	6.3	6.5	6.2	6.4	5.2	6.3
West South Central	9.3	10.4	10.8	10.2	10.4	9.6	10.4
Mountain	4.3	5.1	5.4	5.0	5.3	4.6	5.4
Pacific	13.3	13.6	14.5	14.1	13.7	15.3	13.7
U.S. Total	100.0	100.0	100.0	100.0	100.0	100.0	100.0

SOURCE: Table A.8.

Appendix B

SHIFT-SHARE ANALYSIS

Shift-share analysis separates a region's employment growth in a particular industry into its component sources of growth. The first component is the *national* effect, which reflects overall growth in the national economy. The second component, the *industry* effect, indicates whether employment in a given industry grew faster or slower than overall employment and thus reflects changes in the national industry mix. The regional *shift* effect, which is the third component, reflects differences between the region's industry-specific growth rates and the national industry-specific growth rates.

Shift-share analysis has been used both to analyze past changes in employment and to project future employment.[1] The use of shift-share analysis as a projection technique has been severely criticized, mainly on the grounds that the assumptions required to make the projections are simplistic.[2] Two criticisms of the technique also apply to use of shift-share in historical analyses. First, the relative size of the regional shift factor depends on the number of industry categories used. The smaller the number of categories, the larger the regional factor. This is because the use of aggregated industrial categories obscures the effects of detailed changes in the industrial mix. Second, the use of small time periods may create the illusion that change was underway when only random fluctuations were at work.

Equation (1) presents the shift-share equation. Changes in total employment are decomposed into three components:

$$\Delta E_{ij} = E_{ij}(r..) + E_{ij}(r_i. - r..) + E_{ij}(r_{ij} - r_i.) \tag{1}$$

where E is employment in the base year, i is industry, j is region, and ΔE_{ij} is the change in employment between two years in

155

industry i and region j. The r are employment growth rates ($\Delta E/E$), $r_{..}$ being the national growth rate of total employment, $r_{i.}$ the national growth rate of industry i, and r_{ij} the growth rate of industry i in region j.

The first term in Equation (1) is the *national* effect, and is employment weighted by the growth rate of total employment in the national economy.

The second term in Equation (1) is the *industry* effect, which is employment weighted by the difference between the industry-specific growth rate and the overall national growth rate. Thus, for example, service employment in the United States has been growing much faster than total employment. For service employment in a region $(r_{i.} - r_{..})$ would be positive, and would be the difference between the growth rate of services and the growth rate of total employment in the United States as a whole (from Table 4.3, this would be $43.79 - 25.34 = 18.45$ percent for the 1967–1978 period).

The last factor is the *regional shift* effect. The term in parentheses is, for a *given* industry i, the difference between the regional growth rate and national growth rate. For example, service employment grew faster in the Pacific (73.93 percent between 1967 and 1978, from Appendix Table C.26) than it did in the overall United States (45.79 percent, from Table 4.3). The regional shift effect is thus $73.93 - 43.79 = 30.14$ percent. When the final term in Equation (1) is positive, regional employment in the industry grew faster than national employment in the industry did. When it is negative, growth was slower than the national average.

By definition, for a given industry the sum across regions of the regional component is zero:

$$\sum_j E_{ij} (r_{ij} - r_{i.}) = 0. \tag{2}$$

This is because the growth rate term $(r_{ij} - r_{i.})$ is the regional deviation from the national weighted average.

We focused on employment growth *rates* in our analysis, not the actual employment change. To translate the change into a rate, we divided Equation (1) by E_{ij}. Thus

$$\frac{\Delta E_{ij}}{E_{ij}} = r_{..} + (r_{i.} - r_{..}) + (r_{ij} - r_{i.}). \tag{3}$$

This says that the employment growth rate in a particular industry

and region is the sum of the national growth rate of total employment, the deviation of the growth rate in the particular industry from the national growth rate, and the deviation of the
growth rate in the given industry and region from the national
rate for that particular industry.

The analysis in Chapter 4 emphasized differences in the regional
component (the last term of Equation 3) which we called the
regional industry "shift rate." The tables in Appendix C also present an "annual shift rate" which is simply

$$\frac{(r_{ij} - r_{i.})}{n} \tag{4}$$

where the numerator is the regional shift rate and n is the number
of years in the period we analyzed.

The above discussion pertained to employment growth in a
given region *and* industry. We can also examine total employment
growth in a given region (that is, across all industries). To do this
we sum Equation (1) over the industries:

$$\sum_i \Delta E_{ij} = \sum_i E_{ij}(r..) + \sum_i E_{ij}(r_{i.} - r..) + \sum_i E_{ij}(r_{ij} - r_{i.}). \tag{5}$$

Simplifying and dividing through by $E_{.j}$ (to translate the equation
into rates) we get:

$$\sum_i \frac{\Delta E_{ij}}{E_{.j}} = r.. + \left[\sum_i \frac{E_{ij}}{E_{.j}} (r_{i.} - r..) \right] + \sum_i \frac{E_{ij}}{E_{.j}} (r_{ij} - r_{i.}). \tag{6}$$

This is the calculation we described in the East South Central
example in Chapter 4. Equation (6) thus decomposes the growth
rate of total employment in a region into three components, similar
in interpretation to the components in Equation (3). The first term
is simply the national growth rate.

The second term in Equation (6), the industry effect, has a
slightly different interpretation than it did in Equation (3). It
allows us to assess the impact of a region's industrial mix on its
overall growth. A region has a favorable industrial mix if it has
a lot of employment in rapidly growing industries (services, for
example). A region with an unfavorable mix is one with a high
percentage of employment in slow growing industries (such as
manufacturing). The overall industry effect is positive if the region
has a favorable industry mix and negative if the mix is unfavorable.
The term will be zero if the industry mix in the region is identical
to the national industry mix. We showed in Chapter 4, for ex-

ample, that East South Central, a very rapidly growing region, actually had a slightly unfavorable industry mix.

The regional "shift rate" is the final term in Equation (6). This tells us whether total employment in the region grew faster or slower than one might have expected on the basis of national averages, after adjusting for differences between the regional and national industry mix. Thus, as in Equation (3), the regional shift term captures the regional industry-specific growth rates. In the example in Chapter 4, the regional shift factor in East South Central was positive, indicating that industries in the region grew faster than they did nationally.

Endnotes

1. For examples of the use of shift-share in historical analysis see: Michael R. Greenberg and Nicholas Valenti, "Recent Economic Trends in Major Northeastern Metropolises," in *Post-Industrial America: Metropolitan Decline and Inter-Regional Job Shifts*, ed. Sternlieb and Hughes (New Brunswick, New Jersey: Center for Urban Policy Research, Rutgers University, 1975); and Advisory Commission on Intergovernmental Relations, *Regional Growth: Historic Perspective*, Commission Report A-74 (Washington, D.C.: ACIR, 1980).
2. See: Benjamin Stevens and Craig Moore, "A Critical Review of the Literature of Shift-Share as a Forecasting Technique," Discussion paper No. 109, Regional Science Research Institute, Philadelphia, Pennsylvania, 1978; and H. James Brown, "Shift Share Projections of Regional Growth: Empirical Tests," *Journal of Regional Science*, Vol. 9, No. 1, 1969.

Appendix C

SUPPLEMENTARY TABLES

Table C.1 Back-Up Table for Figure 2.2: Comparison of Actual Growth over 1970–1980 Decade with Census II-B Projections by Age and Region of the Country

	(1) 1970 Base Population	(2) Census II-B Projected Growth 1970–1980	(3) Actual Growth 1970–1980	(4) Difference (3) − (2)	(5) Error in Projected Growth (percent) (4) ÷ (1) × 100
Ages 15–24					
U.S. Total	35,319	6,208	7,155	947	2.68%
New England	2,010	331	309	−22	−1.09
East North Central	6,943	869	966	97	1.40
West North Central	2,814	402	451	49	1.74
Mid-Atlantic	5,966	597	579	−18	−0.30
South Atlantic	5,520	1,285	1,349	64	1.22
East South Central	2,297	309	486	177	7.71
West South Central	3,490	681	1,100	419	12.01
Mountain	1,524	588	678	90	5.91
Pacific	4,755	855	1,238	383	8.05
Ages 25–34					
U.S. Total	24,857	11,315	12,219	904	3.64
New England	1,396	663	600	−63	−4.51
East North Central	4,891	1,907	1,825	−82	−1.68
West North Central	1,872	875	837	−38	−2.03
Mid-Atlantic	4,440	1,383	1,272	−111	−2.50
South Atlantic	3,836	2,092	2,161	69	1.80
East South Central	1,529	739	769	30	1.96
West South Central	2,349	1,296	1,568	272	11.58
Mountain	1,055	704	957	253	24.44
Pacific	3,510	1,505	2,228	723	20.60

Ages 35–44

U.S. Total	23,122	2,599	2,519	−80	−0.35
New England	1,328	114	55	−59	−4.44
East North Central	4,559	205	78	−127	−2.79
West North Central	1,745	156	91	−65	−3.72
Mid-Atlantic	4,398	−26	−201	−184	−4.18
South Atlantic	3,511	705	747	42	1.20
East South Central	1,396	214	233	19	1.36
West South Central	2,157	364	481	117	5.42
Mountain	926	289	357	68	7.34
Pacific	3,103	518	668	150	4.83

Ages 45–54

U.S. Total	23,234	−436	−337	99	0.43
New England	1,397	−110	−126	−16	−1.15
East North Central	4,585	−394	−364	30	0.65
West North Central	1,755	−81	−90	−9	−0.51
Mid-Atlantic	4,614	−494	−583	−89	−1.93
South Atlantic	3,427	291	307	16	0.47
East South Central	1,376	35	64	29	2.11
West South Central	2,043	147	229	82	4.01
Mountain	876	170	164	−6	−0.68
Pacific	3,061	−5	63	68	2.22

Table C.1 (Continued)

	(1) 1970 Base Population	(2) Census II-B Projected Growth 1970–1980	(3) Actual Growth 1970–1980	(4) Difference (3) – (2)	(5) Error in Projected Growth (percent) (4) ÷ (1) × 100
Ages 55–64					
U.S. Total	18,686	2,512	3,014	502	2.69
New England	1,127	132	138	6	0.53
East North Central	3,613	242	373	131	3.63
West North Central	1,544	37	66	29	1.88
Mid-Atlantic	3,768	223	195	−28	−0.74
South Atlantic	2,749	741	874	133	4.84
East South Central	1,188	97	150	53	4.46
West South Central	1,721	223	309	86	5.00
Mountain	679	277	275	−2	−0.29
Pacific	2,298	540	634	94	4.09
Ages 65 +					
U.S. Total	20,092	4,835	5,452	617	3.07
New England	1,271	220	249	29	2.28
East North Central	3,816	570	677	107	2.80
West North Central	1,867	284	332	48	2.57
Mid-Atlantic	3,938	535	613	78	1.98
South Atlantic	2,939	1,331	1,424	93	3.16
East South Central	1,271	332	386	54	4.25
West South Central	1,839	534	624	90	4.89
Mountain	696	329	364	35	5.03
Pacific	2,405	743	832	89	3.70

Table C.2 **Back-Up Table for Figure 2.3: Number of Births by Census Region: Observed Trends, 1965–1980, and Census Series II-B Projections, 1975–1990 (in thousands)**[a]

Region	Actual Trends			Projections		
	1965–1970	1970–1975	1975–1980	1975–1980	1980–1985	1985–1990
New England	1110	884	759	853	1030	1090
East North Central	3622	3467	3102	3229	3716	3757
West North Central	1393	1334	1311	1267	1483	1509
Mid-Atlantic	3130	2778	2399	2563	2969	3042
South Atlantic	2744	2753	2507	2662	3159	3222
East South Central	1213	1216	1152	1122	1268	1280
West South Central	1826	1918	1952	1822	2119	2182
Mountain	779	892	975	892	1086	1146
Pacific	2277	2242	2307	2158	2581	2711
Total U.S.	18,094	17,484	16,464	16,568	19,411	19,939

SOURCES: *Monthly Vital Statistics Reports*, various issues 1967 to 1980; *Current Population Reports*, Series P-25, No. 796.
[a] Estimates for 1965–1970 from January 1, 1965, to December 31, 1969; for 1970–1975 from April 1, 1970, to July 1, 1975; for 1975–1980 from January 1, 1975, to December 31, 1979; for 1980–1985 and 1985–1990 from July 1 to June 30.

Table C.3 Back-Up Table for Figures 2.4a and 2.4b: Population Growth Rates by Regions, 1970–1980 Actual and 1980–1990 Census Projections

Annual Rates of Growth (per 1,000 population)

Region	Actual			Census II-A Projections			Census II-B Projections		
	1965–1970	*1970–1975*	*1975–1980*	*1975–1980*	*1980–1985*	*1985–1990*	*1975–1980*	*1980–1985*	*1985–1990*
New England	11.1	5.4	2.7	6.7	8.6	8.6	6.1	8.1	8.1
East North Central	9.1	3.2	3.5	4.8	6.9	6.8	2.2	4.5	4.5
West North Central	5.0	4.2	5.9	3.6	5.9	5.6	4.0	6.2	6.3
Mid-Atlantic	6.5	0.3	−2.6	1.8	3.9	4.2	0.1	2.3	2.6
South Atlantic	18.1	17.6	19.5	14.1	14.6	13.1	17.1	17.2	15.4
East South Central	7.7	10.2	17.0	7.1	7.4	7.6	8.8	10.1	9.5
West South Central	14.1	14.6	27.5	11.4	12.5	11.6	12.8	13.8	12.7
Mountain	17.2	28.4	36.2	16.5	16.4	14.2	22.6	21.3	17.9
Pacific	20.0	12.0	24.9	12.8	13.8	12.6	11.0	12.1	11.2
Total U.S.	11.9	8.9	12.6	8.1	9.7	9.2	8.1	9.7	9.2

SOURCES: *Current Population Reports*, Series P-25, No. 796; *Advance Reports*, 1980 Census.

Table C.4 Back-Up Table for Figure 3.2: Growth of Metropolitan and Nonmetropolitan Population, 1950–1980

	1950–1960	*1960–1970*	*1970–1980*
Nonmetropolitan Population Growth (%)			
New England	16.7	18.9	13.5
East North Central	11.4	7.4	10.6
West North Central	1.0	− 1.4	4.4
Mid-Atlantic	21.1	17.5	21.9
South Atlantic	15.0	9.9	20.7
East South Central	− 2.4	2.9	14.8
West South Central	− 2.4	4.2	15.6
Mountain	17.0	9.2	35.4
Pacific	24.9	15.4	33.3
Total U.S.	7.1	6.8	15.4
Metropolitan Population Growth (%)			
New England	10.8	12.0	8.0
East North Central	23.8	13.0	1.5
West North Central	24.7	13.1	8.9
Mid-Atlantic	14.4	8.4	− 2.1
South Atlantic	33.7	20.3	11.6
East South Central	24.1	12.4	14.1
West South Central	30.7	18.2	21.0
Mountain	70.4	33.4	34.6
Pacific	34.7	25.2	23.0
Total U.S.	26.4	16.6	9.1

SOURCES: 1960: U.S. Bureau of the Census, *U.S. Census of Population: 1960, General Characteristics* (Washington: GPO, 1963), Figure 39.
1970: U.S. Bureau of the Census, *U.S. Census of the Population: 1970, United States Summary* (Washington: GPO, 1973), Table 42.
1980: preliminary Census data reported in the *New York Times*, March 3, 1981.

Table C.5 Back-Up Table for Figure 3.4: Ratios of Regional to National Total Fertility Rates, 1940–1977

Total Fertility Rate	1940	1950	1960	1970	1971	1972	1973	1974	1975	1976	1977	1978	1979	1980
U.S. Total	2229	3028	3654	2480	2262	2003	1875	1835	1777	1745	1802	1800	1840	1875
New England	2153	2878	3726	2467	2236	1926	1767	1689	1597	1543	1598	NA	NA	NA
East North Central	2191	3067	3793	2540	2310	2014	1880	1824	1766	1704	1767	NA	NA	NA
West North Central	2420	3459	4029	2541	2315	2049	1922	1926	1902	1877	1948	NA	NA	NA
Mid-Atlantic	1796	2557	3368	2396	2125	1853	1726	1668	1614	1574	1611	NA	NA	NA
South Atlantic	2597	3178	3569	2433	2271	2003	1855	1783	1701	1663	1737	NA	NA	NA
East South Central	2992	3564	3727	2623	2488	2225	2094	2021	1951	1893	1984	NA	NA	NA
West South Central	2811	3496	3758	2575	2448	2184	2085	2056	2003	1972	2030	NA	NA	NA
Mountain	2984	3750	4121	2773	2594	2350	2252	2272	2229	2266	2342	NA	NA	NA
Pacific	2069	3172	3940	2552	2314	2100	2977	1985	1941	1950	2011	NA	NA	NA

Ratio to U.S. TFR	1940	1950	1960	1970	1971	1972	1973	1974	1975	1976	1977	1978	1979	1980
U.S. Total	1.00	1.00	1.00	1.00	1.00	1.00	1.00	1.00	1.00	1.00	1.00	1.00	1.00	1.00
New England	0.97	0.95	1.02	0.99	0.99	0.96	0.94	0.92	0.90	0.88	0.89	–	–	–
East North Central	0.98	1.01	1.04	1.02	1.02	1.01	1.00	0.99	0.99	0.98	0.98	–	–	–
West North Central	1.09	1.14	1.10	1.02	1.02	1.02	1.03	1.05	1.07	1.08	1.08	–	–	–
Mid-Atlantic	0.81	0.84	0.92	0.97	0.94	0.93	0.92	0.91	0.91	0.90	0.89	–	–	–
South Atlantic	1.17	1.05	0.98	0.98	1.00	1.00	0.99	0.97	0.96	0.95	0.96	–	–	–
East South Central	1.34	1.18	1.02	1.06	1.10	1.11	1.12	1.10	1.10	1.08	1.10	–	–	–
West South Central	1.26	1.15	1.03	1.04	1.08	1.09	1.11	1.12	1.13	1.13	1.13	–	–	–
Mountain	1.34	1.24	1.13	1.12	1.15	1.17	1.20	1.24	1.25	1.30	1.30	–	–	–
Pacific	0.93	1.05	1.08	1.03	1.02	1.05	1.05	1.08	1.09	1.12	1.12	–	–	–

SOURCE: Martin O'Connell, "Interstate Variations in Birth Expectations," in Hendershot and Placek (eds.), *Predicting Fertility* (Lexington: D.C. Heath, 1981); and unpublished data from U.S. Census Bureau. Regional levels are simple averages of state TFRs.

Table C.6 Back-Up Table for Figure 3.5: Age-Specific Fertility Rates by Race and Region: Average Values for 1970–1975[a]

	Age of Women					
Race and Region	<20	20–24	25–29	30–34	35–39	40+
White and Other						
New England	0.2177	0.6296	0.6273	0.3012	0.1190	0.0373
East North Central	0.2510	0.6565	0.6204	0.3012	0.1194	0.0318
West North Central	0.2421	0.7031	0.6616	0.3121	0.1299	0.0383
Mid-Atlantic	0.1709	0.5518	0.6284	0.3195	0.1219	0.0289
South Atlantic	0.2841	0.5831	0.5465	0.2701	0.1004	0.0235
East South Central	0.3714	0.7183	0.5588	0.2593	0.1022	0.0274
West South Central	0.3626	0.7534	0.5834	0.2608	0.1044	0.0277
Mountain	0.3214	0.8426	0.7141	0.3461	0.1389	0.0402
Pacific	0.2774	0.6928	0.6407	0.3083	0.1141	0.0397
Total U.S.	0.2612	0.6424	0.6061	0.2955	0.1150	0.0297

Black

New England	0.6719	0.8427	0.5593	0.3068	0.1570	0.0476
East North Central	0.7493	0.8817	0.5861	0.3312	0.1663	0.0520
West North Central	0.7897	0.9437	0.5900	0.3410	0.1664	0.0526
Mid-Atlantic	0.5978	0.7858	0.5318	0.2985	0.1387	0.0369
South Atlantic	0.6459	0.7930	0.5169	0.2892	0.1437	0.0468
East South Central	0.7121	0.8804	0.6006	0.3719	0.2215	0.0798
West South Central	0.7141	0.9173	0.6024	0.3634	0.2063	0.0749
Mountain	0.8762	1.0659	0.6872	0.3484	0.1534	0.0749
Pacific	0.6134	0.8389	0.6097	0.3024	0.1341	0.0335
Total U.S.	0.6995	0.8356	0.5584	0.3185	0.1623	0.0514

SOURCE: *Current Population Reports*, Series P-25, No. 796, "Illustrative Projections of State Populations by Age, Race and Sex: 1975 to 2000," Table A-2, p. 130.

[a] Rates represent simple average of state values in each region over the 1970–1975 period.

Table C.7 Back-Up Table for Figure 3.5: Ratio of Regional to National Age-Specific Fertility Rates, 1970–1975 Averages—White and Other Races, Excluding Blacks

	Age of Women					
	<20	20–24	25–29	30–34	35–39	40–44
New England	0.8335	0.9801	1.0350	1.0193	1.0348	1.2559
East North Central	0.9609	1.0219	1.0236	1.0193	1.0383	1.0701
West North Central	0.9269	1.0945	1.0916	1.0562	1.1296	1.2896
Mid-Atlantic	0.6543	0.8589	1.0368	1.0812	1.0600	0.9731
North	0.8429	0.9889	1.0468	1.0440	1.0657	1.1472
South Atlantic	1.0873	0.9077	0.9017	0.9140	0.8730	0.7912
East South Central	1.4219	1.1181	0.9219	0.8775	0.8887	0.9226
West South Central	1.3882	1.1727	0.9625	0.8826	0.9078	0.9327
South	1.2991	1.0662	0.9287	0.8914	0.8898	0.8822
Mountain	1.2305	1.3116	1.1782	1.1712	1.2078	1.3535
Pacific	1.0620	1.0784	1.0571	1.0433	0.9922	1.3367
West	1.1463	1.1950	1.1177	1.1073	1.1000	1.3451
Total U.S.	1.000	1.000	1.000	1.000	1.000	1.000

SOURCE: *Current Population Reports*, Series P-25, No. 796, Table A-2.

Table C.8 **Back-Up Table for Figure 3.6: Population Growth by Age Groups: Observed, 1970–1980, and Census Series II-B Projections, 1980–1990. Total Growth (thousands) and Percent Change**

	Population Growth (thousands)		Percent Change	
Age Group and Region	1970–1980 Observed	1980–1990 Projected	1970–1980 Observed	1980–1990 Projected
15–24				
U.S. Total	7,155	−6,797	20.3	−16.4
New England	309	−450	15.4	−19.2
East North Central	966	−1,703	13.9	−21.8
West North Central	451	−730	16.0	−22.7
Mid-Atlantic	579	−1,433	9.7	−21.8
South Atlantic	1,349	−1,077	24.4	−15.8
East South Central	486	−382	21.2	−14.7
West South Central	1,100	−463	31.6	−11.1
Mountain	678	−161	44.5	−7.6
Pacific	1,238	−797	26.0	−14.2
25–34				
U.S. Total	12,219	4,914	49.2	13.6
New England	600	283	43.0	13.7
East North Central	1,825	659	37.3	9.7
West North Central	837	352	44.7	12.8
Mid-Atlantic	1,272	476	28.6	8.2
South Atlantic	2,161	1,190	56.3	20.1
East South Central	769	284	50.3	12.5
West South Central	1,568	597	66.8	16.4
Mountain	957	422	92.5	24.3
Pacific	2,228	652	63.5	13.0
35–44				
U.S. Total	2,519	10,871	10.9	42.3
New England	55	644	4.1	44.7
East North Central	78	1,788	1.7	37.5
West North Central	91	833	5.2	43.8
Mid-Atlantic	−201	1,327	−4.6	30.4
South Atlantic	747	2,159	21.3	51.2
East South Central	233	746	16.7	46.3
West South Central	481	1,260	22.3	50.0
Mountain	357	622	38.6	54.5
Pacific	668	1,451	21.5	40.1

Table C.8 (Continued)

Age Group and Region	Population Growth (thousands)		Percent Change	
	1970–1980 Observed	1980–1990 Projected	1970–1980 Observed	1980–1990 Projected
45–54				
U.S. Total	− 337	2,613	− 1.5	11.5
New England	− 126	123	− 9.0	9.6
East North Central	− 364	252	− 7.9	6.0
West North Central	− 90	166	− 5.1	9.9
Mid-Atlantic	− 583	19	− 12.6	0.5
South Atlantic	307	834	9.0	22.4
East South Central	64	208	4.7	14.7
West South Central	229	464	11.2	21.2
Mountain	164	263	18.7	25.1
Pacific	63	504	2.1	16.5
55–64				
U.S. Total	3,014	− 442	16.1	− 2.0
New England	138	− 97	12.2	− 7.7
East North Central	373	− 327	10.3	− 8.5
West North Central	66	− 78	4.3	− 4.9
Mid-Atlantic	195	− 412	5.2	− 10.3
South Atlantic	874	241	31.8	6.9
East South Central	150	28	12.6	2.2
West South Central	309	122	18.0	6.3
Mountain	275	124	40.5	13.0
Pacific	634	− 25	27.5	− 0.9
65 +				
U.S. Total	5,452	4,898	27.1	19.6
New England	249	235	19.6	15.8
East North Central	677	573	17.7	13.1
West North Central	332	164	17.8	7.6
Mid-Atlantic	613	142	15.6	3.2
South Atlantic	1,424	1,382	48.5	32.4
East South Central	386	281	30.4	17.5
West South Central	624	483	33.9	20.4
Mountain	364	393	52.3	38.3
Pacific	832	851	34.6	27.0

SOURCE: 1970 and 1980 Census; and *Current Population Reports*, Series P-25, No. 796, "Illustrative Projections of State Populations by Age, Race and Sex: 1975–2000."

Table C.9   New England: Industrial Mix for Selected Years

Industry	Percent Employed			
	1967	*1970*	*1974*	*1978*
Total Wage and Salary Employment	100.00	100.00	100.00	100.00
Agriculture, Forestry, Fisheries	1.19	1.08	1.00	0.76
Mining	0.06	0.07	0.05	0.06
Construction	4.23	4.55	4.07	3.37
Manufacturing	33.24	29.72	28.12	27.39
Transportation	1.69	2.17	1.50	1.38
Communications	1.23	1.40	1.47	1.24
Public Utilities	0.82	0.82	0.81	0.73
Wholesale and Retail Trade	18.35	19.55	20.20	20.89
Finance, Insurance, and Real Estate	4.77	5.16	5.53	5.61
Services	17.52	18.33	19.83	21.97
Government	16.89	17.16	17.42	16.61

Table C.10 New England: Selected Measures of Employment Growth by Industry, 1967–1978

Industry	1967 Employment	Actual Percent Change 1967–1978	Shift 1967–1978	Annual Shift Rate (percent)			
				1967–1978	1967–1970	1970–1974	1974–1978
Total Wage and Salary Employment	4,669,221	15.22	−448,687	−0.87	−0.47	−1.14	−0.70
Agriculture, Forestry, Fisheries	55,776	−26.43	−18,306	−2.98	−0.47	−2.07	−6.32
Mining	2,936	8.04	−671	−2.08	3.74	−6.33	−1.21
Construction	197,518	−8.35	−72,183	−3.32	1.89	−4.69	−4.97
Manufacturing	1,552,093	−5.07	−171,631	−1.01	−2.10	−1.01	−0.12
Transportation	78,920	−5.98	−10,372	−1.19	10.51	7.70	−1.06
Communications	57,501	16.10	−7,038	−1.11	0.75	0.68	−3.50
Public Utilities	38,102	2.43	−6,525	−1.56	−0.59	−1.44	−2.06
Wholesale and Retail Trade	856,926	31.14	−91,060	−0.97	0.28	−1.17	−1.21
Finance, Insurance, and Real Estate	222,610	35.51	−22,889	−0.93	−0.09	−1.12	−0.85
Services	818,049	44.51	5,878	0.07	−0.07	−0.35	0.56
Government	788,790	13.31	−53,890	−0.62	−0.36	−0.45	−0.81

Table C.11   Mid-Atlantic: Industrial Mix for Selected Years

Industry	*Percent Employed*			
	1967	*1970*	*1974*	*1978*
Total Wage and Salary Employment	100.00	100.00	100.00	100.00
Agriculture, Forestry, Fisheries	0.72	0.65	0.75	0.78
Mining	0.36	0.34	0.12	0.38
Construction	3.97	4.01	3.90	3.34
Manufacturing	30.18	28.02	25.59	24.01
Transportation	4.20	3.97	3.69	3.52
Communications	1.42	1.62	1.55	1.50
Public Utilities	0.89	0.89	0.89	0.87
Wholesale and Retail Trade	18.61	19.18	19.65	20.51
Finance, Insurance, and Real Estate	5.80	6.26	6.40	6.50
Services	17.68	18.04	19.58	21.62
Government	16.17	17.03	17.89	16.98

Table C.12 Mid-Atlantic: Selected Measures of Employment Growth by Industry, 1967–1978

Industry	1967 Employment	Actual Percent Change 1967–1978	Shift 1967–1978	Annual Shift Rate (percent)			
				1967–1978	1967–1970	1970–1974	1974–1978
Total Wage and Salary Employment	14,343,760	5.66	−2,829,160	−1.79	−0.83	−1.88	−1.98
Agriculture, Forestry, Fisheries	102,565	15.65	9,496	0.84	−0.49	2.80	−0.05
Mining	51,621	10.38	−10,593	−1.87	−0.03	−18.87	51.46
Construction	570,102	−11.33	−225,353	−3.59	−0.70	−3.42	−5.28
Manufacturing	4,328,832	−15.92	−948,429	−1.99	−1.18	−2.54	−2.26
Transportation	602,270	−11.34	−111,452	−1.68	−1.57	−2.13	−1.38
Communications	203,861	11.65	−34,019	−1.52	0.64	−2.43	−1.51
Public Utilities	127,695	3.67	−20,285	−1.44	−1.07	−1.75	−1.13
Wholesale and Retail Trade	2,669,327	16.44	−675,870	−2.30	−1.20	−2.15	−2.31
Finance, Insurance, and Real Estate	831,358	18.41	−227,665	−2.49	−0.50	−3.12	−2.16
Services	2,536,615	29.15	−371,298	−1.33	−1.27	−1.06	−0.97
Government	2,319,514	10.93	−213,690	−0.84	0.64	−0.30	−2.16

Table C.13   East North Central: Industrial Mix for Selected Years

| | Percent Employed | | | |
Industry	1967	1970	1974	1978
Total Wage and Salary Employment	100.00	100.00	100.00	100.00
Agriculture, Forestry, Fisheries	1.15	1.04	1.14	1.23
Mining	0.45	0.36	0.40	0.41
Construction	4.31	4.20	3.80	3.95
Manufacturing	34.62	32.67	31.36	29.48
Transportation	3.44	3.31	3.12	2.96
Communications	1.15	1.27	1.22	1.12
Public Utilities	0.88	0.92	0.89	0.86
Wholesale and Retail Trade	19.26	20.04	20.35	21.22
Finance, Insurance, and Real Estate	4.05	4.28	4.50	4.67
Services	14.69	15.24	16.41	17.95
Government	15.99	16.68	16.79	16.14

Table C.14 East North Central: Selected Measures of Employment Growth by Industry, 1967–1978

Industry	1967 Employment	Actual Percent Change 1967–1978	Shift 1967–1978	Annual Shift Rate (percent)			
				1967–1978	1967–1970	1970–1974	1974–1978
Total Wage and Salary Employment	14,886,684	17.33	−963,290	−0.59	−0.55	−0.44	−0.56
Agriculture, Forestry, Fisheries	171,464	24.94	31,796	1.69	−0.61	2.99	1.99
Mining	67,563	6.81	−16,281	−2.19	−4.59	1.78	−3.28
Construction	641,080	7.64	−131,814	−1.87	−1.79	−3.88	0.72
Manufacturing	5,154,175	−0.10	−313,834	−0.55	−0.56	−0.09	−0.98
Transportation	512,676	0.97	−31,735	−0.56	−0.92	−0.54	−0.27
Communications	171,676	14.25	−24,183	−1.28	−0.56	−1.14	−1.46
Public Utilities	130,903	14.65	−6,432	−0.45	0.45	−1.05	−0.38
Wholesale and Retail Trade	2,866,906	29.28	−357,867	−1.13	−0.76	−1.04	−0.95
Finance, Insurance, and Real Estate	603,079	35.29	−63,383	−0.96	−1.22	−1.02	−0.17
Services	2,186,944	43.39	−8,708	−0.04	−0.58	0.16	0.22
Government	2,380,218	18.42	−40,849	−0.16	0.40	−0.09	−0.57

Table C.15 West North Central: Industrial Mix for Selected Years

Industry	Percent Employed			
	1967	*1970*	*1974*	*1978*
Total Wage and Salary Employment	100.00	100.00	100.00	100.00
Agriculture, Forestry, Fisheries	3.24	2.72	2.95	2.73
Mining	0.70	0.70	0.64	0.58
Construction	4.55	4.47	4.33	4.77
Manufacturing	21.93	20.68	19.44	19.48
Transportation	4.17	3.93	3.92	3.71
Communications	1.29	1.35	1.31	1.28
Public Utilities	1.01	0.98	0.94	0.90
Wholesale and Retail Trade	21.18	22.02	22.70	23.69
Finance, Insurance, and Real Estate	4.39	4.50	4.76	4.96
Services	16.30	16.75	18.02	18.42
Government	21.24	21.90	21.00	19.48

Table C.16 West North Central: Selected Measures of Employment Growth by Industry, 1967–1978

Industry	1967 Employment	Actual Percent Change 1967–1978	Shift 1967–1978	Annual Shift Rate (percent)			
				1967–1978	1967–1970	1970–1974	1974–1978
Total Wage and Salary Employment	5,617,772	27.01	48,408	0.08	−0.15	0.03	0.34
Agriculture, Forestry, Fisheries	181,977	7.13	1,345	0.07	−2.19	3.13	−0.89
Mining	39,603	5.19	−10,184	−2.34	2.50	−2.73	−5.27
Construction	255,422	33.21	12,799	0.46	−0.82	−1.67	3.53
Manufacturing	1,232,120	12.82	84,231	0.62	0.03	−0.06	1.71
Transportation	234,181	12.90	13,447	0.52	−0.91	1.45	0.63
Communications	72,746	25.11	−2,346	−0.29	−2.05	−0.20	0.97
Public Utilities	56,694	13.00	−3,721	−0.60	−1.40	−0.98	0.55
Wholesale and Retail Trade	1,189,606	42.10	4,000	0.03	−0.10	−0.02	0.17
Finance, Insurance, and Real Estate	246,410	43.75	−5,030	−0.19	−1.63	−0.19	1.04
Services	915,678	43.50	−2,661	−0.03	−0.23	0.76	−0.63
Government	1,193,335	16.50	−43,471	−0.33	0.65	−0.78	−0.50

Table C.17   South Atlantic: Industrial Mix for Selected Years

Industry	*Percent Employed*			
	1967	*1970*	*1974*	*1978*
Total Wage and Salary Employment	100.00	100.00	100.00	100.00
Agriculture, Forestry, Fisheries	2.92	2.41	2.17	2.19
Mining	0.72	0.71	0.72	0.33
Construction	5.26	5.55	6.33	5.45
Manufacturing	22.42	21.75	20.72	20.17
Transportation	3.17	3.23	2.94	2.87
Communications	1.26	1.41	1.43	1.37
Public Utilities	0.77	0.82	0.83	0.79
Wholesale and Retail Trade	17.43	18.46	19.28	20.69
Finance, Insurance, and Real Estate	3.90	4.27	4.84	4.88
Services	16.94	16.78	17.21	16.68
Government	25.21	24.61	23.53	24.59

Table C.18 South Atlantic: Selected Measures of Employment Growth by Industry, 1967–1978

Industry	1967 Employment	Actual Percent Change 1967–1978	Shift 1967–1978	Annual Shift Rate (percent)				
				1967–1978	1967–1970	1970–1974	1974–1978
Total Wage and Salary Employment	11,130,370	31.50	664,779	0.54	0.81	1.40	−0.70
Agriculture, Forestry, Fisheries	325,461	−1.63	−26,114	−0.73	−1.95	−0.64	0.25
Mining	79,716	−38.89	−55,638	−6.35	3.70	1.29	−18.37
Construction	585,111	36.27	47,245	0.73	2.71	4.58	−4.08
Manufacturing	2,494,992	18.35	308,484	1.12	1.89	1.62	−0.17
Transportation	353,254	18.83	41,227	1.06	2.71	0.32	0.37
Communications	139,690	43.73	21,510	1.40	1.79	2.46	−0.53
Public Utilities	86,230	33.80	12,279	1.29	2.46	2.13	−0.78
Wholesale and Retail Trade	1,939,752	56.11	278,399	1.30	1.58	1.80	−0.22
Finance, Insurance and Real Estate	434,351	64.35	80,572	1.69	1.80	3.45	−1.07
Services	1,885,740	29.44	−270,572	−1.30	−0.61	0.82	−3.18
Government	2,806,073	28.24	227,387	0.74	−0.37	0.47	1.57

Table C.19   East South Central: Industrial Mix for Selected Years

Industry	Percent Employed			
	1967	1970	1974	1978
Total Wage and Salary Employment	100.00	100.00	100.00	100.00
Agriculture, Forestry, Fisheries	3.87	3.22	2.69	2.34
Mining	1.01	0.91	1.22	1.51
Construction	4.74	4.54	5.13	5.02
Manufacturing	26.49	27.41	26.00	25.55
Transportation	3.01	2.74	2.85	2.74
Communications	1.08	1.19	1.23	1.24
Public Utilities	0.66	0.69	0.71	0.72
Wholesale and Retail Trade	16.49	17.05	18.08	19.25
Finance, Insurance, and Real Estate	3.19	3.39	3.82	3.84
Services	17.53	17.15	16.88	17.22
Government	21.95	21.72	21.38	20.56

Table C.20 East South Central: Selected Measures of Employment Growth by Industry, 1967-1978

Industry	1967 Employment	Actual Percent Change 1967-1978	Shift 1967-1978	Annual Shift Rate (percent)			
				1967-1978	1967-1970	1970-1974	1974-1978
Total Wage and Salary Employment	4,243,810	30.77	263,075	0.56	-0.20	0.79	0.80
Agriculture, Forestry, Fisheries	164,049	-20.80	-44,607	-2.47	-2.66	-3.06	-2.13
Mining	42,873	95.96	27,892	5.91	-0.79	9.83	4.00
Construction	201,108	38.42	20,557	0.93	-1.95	3.48	0.43
Manufacturing	1,124,103	26.15	226,623	1.83	3.01	0.81	1.50
Transportation	127,939	18.81	14,896	1.06	-2.32	3.31	1.37
Communications	45,728	50.95	10,340	2.06	-0.24	2.27	2.35
Public Utilities	27,808	43.90	6,770	2.21	1.11	1.95	2.29
Wholesale and Retail Trade	699,618	52.70	76,550	0.99	-0.57	1.51	1.10
Finance, Insurance, and Real Estate	135,318	57.52	15,863	1.07	-0.60	2.49	0.30
Services	743,825	28.51	-113,656	-1.39	-2.21	-1.05	-0.35
Government	931,441	22.48	21,847	0.21	-1.04	0.57	0.74

Table C.21   West South Central: Industrial Mix for Selected Years

Industry	Percent Employed			
	1967	1970	1974	1978
Total Wage and Salary Employment	100.00	100.00	100.00	100.00
Agriculture, Forestry, Fisheries	3.57	3.23	2.46	2.25
Mining	3.09	2.81	2.75	3.38
Construction	5.77	5.44	6.00	6.61
Manufacturing	16.93	17.32	17.00	16.91
Transportation	3.93	3.66	3.83	3.40
Communications	1.17	1.28	1.35	1.32
Public Utilities	1.15	1.14	1.13	1.05
Wholesale and Retail Trade	19.56	20.46	21.30	22.33
Finance, Insurance, and Real Estate	4.01	4.33	4.83	4.82
Services	17.88	18.03	17.81	18.23
Government	22.94	22.30	21.53	19.69

Table C.22 West South Central: Selected Measures of Employment Growth by Industry, 1967–1978

Industry	1967 Employment	Actual Percent Change 1967–1978	Shift 1967–1978	Annual Shift Rate (percent)			
				1967–1978	1967–1970	1970–1974	1974–1978
Total Wage and Salary Employment	6,498,845	41.44	930,723	1.30	0.08	0.98	2.02
Agriculture, Forestry, Fisheries	231,693	–10.87	–39,989	–1.57	0.36	–4.78	0.33
Mining	200,593	55.06	48,465	2.20	–0.08	0.16	5.52
Construction	375,139	61.84	126,209	3.06	–2.06	3.20	5.46
Manufacturing	1,100,506	41.26	388,151	3.21	3.10	2.13	3.26
Transportation	255,324	22.55	39,291	1.40	–1.04	3.92	0.59
Communications	76,305	59.58	23,840	2.84	–0.02	3.17	2.90
Public Utilities	74,657	29.13	7,149	0.87	–0.47	1.15	1.29
Wholesale and Retail Trade	1,271,139	61.49	250,806	1.79	0.38	1.39	2.13
Finance, Insurance, and Real Estate	260,315	70.34	63,886	2.23	0.58	2.56	1.59
Services	1,162,295	44.17	4,473	0.03	–0.66	–0.57	1.22
Government	1,490,879	21.38	18,441	0.11	–1.17	0.43	0.73

Table C.23   Mountain: Industrial Mix for Selected Years

Industry	Percent Employed			
	1967	1970	1974	1978
Total Wage and Salary Employment	100.00	100.00	100.00	100.00
Agriculture, Forestry, Fisheries	4.43	3.63	2.90	2.72
Mining	2.89	2.48	2.66	2.74
Construction	5.04	5.35	6.38	6.78
Manufacturing	11.87	12.01	12.05	11.78
Transportation	3.19	2.98	2.77	2.25
Communications	1.57	1.57	1.60	1.50
Public Utilities	1.26	1.17	1.16	1.15
Wholesale and Retail Trade	20.98	20.99	21.76	22.82
Finance, Insurance, and Real Estate	4.18	4.32	4.87	4.97
Services	14.62	17.26	17.47	19.01
Government	29.95	28.22	26.39	24.29

Table C.24 Mountain: Selected Measures of Employment Growth by Industry, 1967–1978

Industry	1967 Employment	Actual Percent Change 1967–1978	Shift 1967–1978	Annual Shift Rate (percent)			
				1967–1978	1967–1970	1970–1974	1974–1978
Total Wage and Salary Employment	2,583,337	68.34	1,059,212	3.73	2.95	3.18	2.49
Agriculture, Forestry, Fisheries	114,570	3.15	−3,712	−0.29	−0.27	−1.93	1.53
Mining	74,699	59.33	21,233	2.58	0.65	5.13	0.18
Construction	130,103	126.52	127,922	8.94	5.39	8.38	4.85
Manufacturing	306,742	67.05	187,293	5.55	5.74	5.01	3.22
Transportation	82,472	18.43	9,290	1.02	1.74	2.74	−1.28
Communications	40,576	60.48	13,045	2.92	−0.32	4.53	2.00
Public Utilities	32,632	53.17	10,969	3.06	−0.04	3.38	3.62
Wholesale and Retail Trade	542,017	83.12	224,177	3.76	1.76	3.60	2.65
Finance, Insurance, and Real Estate	108,104	99.74	58,317	4.90	2.02	5.40	2.67
Services	377,707	118.90	283,701	6.83	8.99	2.40	3.64
Government	773,715	36.55	126,977	1.49	0.58	1.69	1.36

Table C.25   Pacific: Industrial Mix for Selected Years

Industry	Percent Employed			
	1967	*1970*	*1974*	*1978*
Total Wage and Salary Employment	100.00	100.00	100.00	100.00
Agriculture, Forestry, Fisheries	3.14	3.23	3.35	3.08
Mining	0.39	0.32	0.34	0.33
Construction	4.06	4.07	4.02	4.45
Manufacturing	21.55	19.21	18.85	18.20
Transportation	3.48	3.37	3.21	2.94
Communications	1.66	1.74	1.59	1.52
Public Utilities	0.75	0.73	0.72	0.64
Wholesale and Retail Trade	19.10	19.76	20.46	21.63
Finance, Insurance, and Real Estate	4.61	4.96	5.30	5.58
Services	16.40	17.97	18.76	20.49
Government	24.86	24.66	23.40	21.13

Table C.26 Pacific: Selected Measures of Employment Growth by Industry, 1967–1978

Industry	1967 Employment	Actual Percent Change 1967–1978	Shift 1967–1978	Annual Shift Rate (percent)			
				1967–1978	1967–1970	1970–1974	1974–1978
Total Wage and Salary Employment	9,563,075	39.23	1,274,940	1.21	0.71	0.37	1.84
Agriculture, Forestry, Fisheries	300,694	36.35	90,092	2.72	5.32	2.27	0.28
Mining	37,217	19.56	−4,222	−1.03	−2.50	1.68	−2.05
Construction	388,417	52.56	94,618	2.21	0.67	−0.68	5.31
Manufacturing	2,060,732	17.59	239,111	1.05	−0.99	1.48	2.11
Transportation	332,847	17.80	35,408	0.97	0.79	0.69	1.18
Communications	158,917	27.61	−1,148	−0.07	−0.96	−1.39	1.97
Public Utilities	71,279	19.27	−204	−0.03	−0.38	0.24	−0.02
Wholesale and Retail Trade	1,826,709	57.68	290,866	1.45	0.63	0.54	2.10
Finance, Insurance, and Real Estate	440,455	68.57	100,330	2.07	1.14	0.56	2.81
Services	1,568,773	73.93	472,842	2.74	3.13	0.33	2.91
Government	2,377,035	18.34	−42,753	−0.16	0.16	−0.65	0.13

Table C.27   Wage and Salary Income of Full-Time Equivalent Workers as a Percentage of the National Average

	Year						
Region	*1958*	*1961*	*1964*	*1967*	*1970*	*1973*	*1977*
New England	96	96	97	98	98	98	95
Mid-Atlantic	107	108	108	108	109	110	109
East North Central	108	107	107	106	105	107	106
West North Central	92	93	92	92	92	91	92
South Atlantic	87	86	87	88	91	92	92
East South Central	80	79	79	81	82	83	85
West South Central	88	87	86	88	89	88	94
Mountain	100	100	99	96	95	95	96
Pacific	114	116	115	114	111	108	109

SOURCE: Lynn E. Browne, "Changing Regional Labor Markets," doctoral thesis, Massachusetts Institute of Technology, Cambridge, Mass., September 1980, p. 127.

Table C.28   Labor-Force Participation Relative to National Averages, 1960–1978

Region	*1960*	*1971*	*1976*	*1978*
New England	104	104	105	103
Mid-Atlantic	101	96	96	95
East North Central	101	101	102	102
West North Central	99	103	104	104
South Atlantic	100	100	100	99
East South Central	93	97	96	95
West South Central	96	100	99	99
Mountain	100	102	103	102
Pacific	103	100	102	103
U.S. Total	100	100	100	100

INDEX

Urban life, regional effects of,
    131–132
Utah, nonwhite population in, 91
Utilities, employment growth in,
    98, 99, 100

Vermont
    demographics of, 51
    immigration to, 47
    population projections for, 37

Wages (*see also* Earnings)
    regional differentiation in, 41,
        121
    regional trends in, 125–126
Washington, D.C., hispanic popula-
    tion in, 90
Water, regional concentrations of,
    127
Waterways, importance of, 3
West
    and changing age structure, 79,
        82
    employment growth in, 103
    fertility patterns in, 74, 75, 76
    meaning of, 8
    and power shifts, 2
West North Central region
    birth rates for, 35
    changing racial and ethnic mix in,
        88–91
    employment growth in, 102, 103,
        104–105, 107
    industrial mix in, 106
    and interregional migration,
        68–73
    meaning of, 9
    metropolitan vs. nonmetropolitan
        growth in, 66
    during 1970s, 14
    nonagricultural employment in,
        96
    per-capita income in, 112
    population of, 28, 29, 152
    population growth in, 54, 55, 58,
        60

population projections for, 26, 27,
    46, 62–64, 152, 153–154
projected earnings for, 139, 142,
    148
projected employment for, 143,
    149–151
resurgent growth in, 45
West South Central region
    birth rates for, 35
    and changing age structure, 79,
        82
    changing racial and ethnic mix in,
        88–91
    employment growth in, 104–105
    fast-growth economy of, 41
    fertility patterns in, 74, 75, 123
    industrial mix in, 108–109
    and interregional migration,
        68–73
    manufacturing employment in, 97
    metropolitan vs. nonmetropolitan
        growth in, 66
    during 1970s, 14
    nonagricultural employment in,
        96
    per-capita income in, 112
    population of, 28, 29, 152
    population growth in, 54
    population projections for, 26, 27,
        62–64, 146, 152, 153–154
    projected earnings for, 139, 142,
        148
    projected employment for, 143,
        149–151
    projected housing structure for,
        129
Workers, migration of, 17–18 (*see
    also* Labor force participation)
Working conditions, regional effects
    of, 130–131
Working rate
    defined, 111
    interregional variation in,
        115–117

Zero-Sum Society, The (Thurow),
    133